SURVIVE the Bomb

The Radioactive Citizen's Guide to Nuclear Survival

Edited by Eric G. Swedin

ZENITH PRESS

Eric G. Swedin is an associate professor at Weber State University and the author of seven books, including *When Angels Wept: A What-If History of the Cuban Missile Crisis*. He lives near Ogden, Utah.

First published in 2011 by Zenith Press, an imprint of MBI Publishing Company, 400 1st Avenue North, Suite 300, Minneapolis, MN 55401 USA.

Zenith Press titles are also available at discounts in bulk quantity for industrial or sales-promotional use. For details write to Special Sales Manager at MBI Publishing Company, 400 First Avenue North, Suite 300, Minneapolis, MN 55401 USA.

To find out more about our books, join us online at www.zenithpress.com.

Cover design: Angel Bomb Design
Interior design: John Sticha
Additional editing and research: Steve Gansen, Zenith Press

© Shutterstock, p. 3, 15, 21, 27, 33, 45, 47, 56

Editor's note: Some of the government documents in this compilation have been abridged and lightly edited for readability. For instance, footnote numbers and various other cross references have been adjusted for clarity and to maintain sequential numbering.

Library of Congress Cataloging-in-Publication Data

Survive the bomb : the radioactive citizen's guide to nuclear survival / edited by Eric G. Swedin.
    p. cm.
 ISBN-13: 978-0-7603-4031-8
 ISBN-10: 0-7603-4031-5
1. Civil defense—United States—History—20th century.
2. Nuclear warfare—Social aspects—United States.
3. Atomic bomb—Safety measures. I. Swedin, Eric Gottfrid.
 UA927.S934 2011
 613.6'9—dc22

             2010041622

Printed in the United States of America

Contents

Introduction

Attention Fellow Citizens!

In this day of full-body screens and groin pat-downs performed in hopes of preventing another terrorist from trying to light his shoes on fire, it is tempting to imagine that the yesteryear of the 1950s and 1960s was a kinder, simpler time.

Tempting, but false.

Those were the days, after all, when basement food pantries were converted into cinderblock bomb shelters. It was a time when mothers panicked if they saw children catching snowflakes on their tongues (radioactive fallout contaminated snow as far away as five hundred miles from atomic test blasts) and when schoolkids had fallout drills first thing in the morning (right after pledging allegiance to the flag).

A simpler time? Maybe, but it had its share of paranoid insanity, and the craziness is on full display here. *Survive the Bomb: The Radioactive Citizen's Guide to Nuclear Survival* contains just some of the artifacts documenting a nationwide panic that lingered for decades. It might have been the first prolonged doomsday panic, but it probably won't be the last.

Baby boomers and the adults who raised them have long reflected on the years following World War II as a golden era for peace and prosperity in the United States. Fascism had just been defeated on a global scale, and the American free market system was working at full capacity. This prosperity was aided by suburban sprawl, which coincided with the growth of an interstate highway system championed by President Dwight D. Eisenhower. Ike was well aware of the necessity to modernize America's roadways into sophisticated ground transport routes in the case of a military emergency. The cause gained even more political momentum as anxiety about nuclear war grew.

In the early 1950s, fantastic notions of what the atom could unleash started to appear in such films as *The Beast from 20,000 Fathoms*, *Them!*, *This Island Earth*, and a series of movies featuring a giant lizard awakened by atomic tests, Godzilla, courtesy of Japan's Toho Studios. Japan was clearly back on its feet, exporting its own radioactive monster to the nation that less than a decade prior had dropped atomic bombs on two of its cities. That the Japanese had transmuted the most horrific event in their history into mass entertainment for the responsible country has a wonderfully perverse feel to it.

But then, so does our modern fascination with the Atomic Age, doesn't it?

Perhaps those atomic sci-fi films in the early 1950s were America's way to mentally process its own impending nuclear catastrophe. Atomic anxiety among U.S. citizens would hit its stride in the form of the Cold War. With Russia's launch of *Sputnik* in 1957, a switch flipped in the American imagination, transforming mutated monster fantasies to the very real fear of nuclear annihilation.

It all looks so quaint in hindsight. This was partly by design. The children of that generation will remember Bert the Turtle, who instructed them how to "duck and cover." They will remember when regular tests of the Emergency Broadcast System interrupted their Saturday morning cartoons, and when part of any family's survival plan included tuning into CONELRAD* radio—640 or 1240 on the AM dial—for further instructions. *Survive the Bomb* documents other U.S. government efforts to calm the collective psyche with fallout shelter plans, educational comic books, and informational packets handed out by schools or available from civil defense agencies.

Cheerful and naïve representations like those on the following pages have been credited with inspiring more skeptical schoolchildren to question authority at an early age. A counterculture was born, beginning with beatniks and culminating with Woodstock and antiwar protests in the following decades. It recalls the character in the movie *Animal House*, an ROTC student who stands amid a frantic mob, struggling to calm the riot with his whistle and shouts of "All is well, remain calm!" Of course, he is eventually trampled and flattened under the stampeding horde.

This strange era reached its peak in 1962 with the Cuban Missile Crisis, lasting at least until the fall of the Berlin Wall. The nightmare lingers today with terrorist threats of dirty bombs and

---

* Control of Electromagnetic Radiation; CONELRAD could be invoked by the commander of North American Air Defense as the principal means of keeping the public informed in case of attack.

efforts by countries like Iran and North Korea to build their own nuclear arsenals.

Is it premature to think of this nightmare as a finite thing of the past? Could the following whimsical return to the early Atomic Age turn out to be a practical guide for a future unthinkable event? Maybe we should not be so quick to mock those who take our guide for nuclear survival to heart. Maybe they will be the ones who are laughing when their ill-prepared neighbors are pounding away for entry into their cozy, well-stocked shelters during some future dystopian reality.

Those who aren't so self-sufficient can only hope that these savvy citizens will be willing to share their emergency drinking water and freeze-dried meats, if not their shelter. But, undoubtedly, supplies—and space—will be limited.

All is well, remain calm. . . .

The fireball of the world's first hydrogen bomb blossoms over the Pacific, exploded by the Americans on a small island at Eniwetok Atoll, November 1, 1952. The island disappeared, leaving a mile-wide crater 175 feet deep.

This successful test was the culmination of an effort to upgrade the U.S. nuclear arsenal after reports of the first Soviet atomic bomb test in August 1949. This prompted American war planners to finally agree on an idea that had been promoted by famed physicist Edward Teller ever since the Manhattan Project: a superbomb based on fusion, rather than fission. It would be called a hydrogen bomb, rather than an atomic bomb.

The process of nuclear fusion combines atomic nuclei rather than splitting them apart like nuclear fission, and fusion releases even more energy than fission does—a lot more. While the yield of atomic bombs is measured in kilotons, the measurement of hydrogen bombs is measured in megatons (the equivalent of millions of tons of TNT). "Little Boy," the bomb dropped on Hiroshima, had a yield of 15 kilotons; the bomb exploded in this photo had a yield of 10.4 megatons.

After this successful test, Teller became known as the "father of the hydrogen bomb." The Soviets would explode their first hydrogen bomb nine months later, and the nuclear arms race accelerated. *United States Atomic Energy Commission*

I.
The Fallout of Sputnik
1957–1959

World War II was the first nuclear war, and we hope that it will be the last. It was also the most destructive war in history, and one of the causes of destruction came from great armadas of strategic bombers attempting to win the war on their own by destroying the enemy. What was the difference between destroying a city with a single bomb or tens of thousands of bombs? Many people seemed to sense that the atomic bomb changed everything: it was not just a big bomb, but in sufficient numbers, it was a civilization killer.

Even though the war was over, the United States continued to build more atomic bombs. The Cold War developed in the late 1940s, a global ideological struggle between communism, led by the Soviet Union, and democracy and free markets, led by the United States and its Western European allies. Both antagonists realized how important science and technology were to their efforts, and funding levels for research into science and technology continued at unprecedented levels during the Cold War.

The Soviet Union, though considered a scientific and technological backwater, became the second nation to develop an atomic bomb. Exploding their first bomb in 1949, the Soviets shocked the Americans, who had assumed that their superweapon monopoly would last longer. The Soviet Union, deeply committed to the Cold War, was willing to spend the enormous resources necessary to develop nuclear weapons. A strong traditional academic emphasis on mathematics and physics among Soviet scientists allowed the Soviets to catch up, though they were also helped by information supplied by multiple spies in the Manhattan Project. The first Soviet atomic bomb was a copy of the American Fat Man design.

A watershed moment credited with igniting the space age and truly heating up the Cold War was, of course, Russia's launch of a tiny satellite called *Sputnik* on October 4, 1957. The propaganda value to the Soviet Union was enormous, but its real effect was to awaken a half-asleep United States giant, ushering in an era of out-of-control nuclear proliferation between the world's two military superpowers.

The Soviet Union had started building the first civilian nuclear power plant in 1954, with the United Kingdom following a year later, and the United States started building its first civilian reactor in 1956. Nuclear reactors to power submarines and ships, giving them effectively unlimited fuel and range, were also developed. The first nuclear-powered American submarine, USS *Nautilus*, was launched in 1954. The Soviets launched a nuclear-powered icebreaker in 1959. The Americans launched the USS *Long Beach*, a nuclear-powered cruiser, in 1961, and over the next several decades, all of the submarines and many of the larger ships in the American navy came to rely on nuclear power as older craft were replaced by newer designs. Other experimental vessels developed by the Americans included a nuclear-powered airplane, a nuclear-powered merchant freighter, and a nuclear-powered rocket, none of which proved practical.

The following section contains much of the Federal Civil Defense Administration's 1958 report, demonstrating a concerted effort to mobilize all levels of government, emergency services, the business community, schools, the civilian populace—even churches and labor unions—into one all-encompassing nuclear disaster plan.

This section also contains a couple of interesting artifacts mentioned in the report: an excerpt from the educational comic book *Operation Survival*, a wallet card with family preparedness instructions, and information on warning signals that was distributed to 25 million citizens.

ANNUAL REPORT

of the

Federal Civil Defense Administration

for

FISCAL YEAR 1958

EXECUTIVE OFFICE OF THE PRESIDENT
OFFICE OF CIVIL AND DEFENSE MOBILIZATION

UNITED STATES GOVERNMENT PRINTING OFFICE: 1959

For sale by the Superintendent of Documents, U.S. Government Printing Office
Washington 25, D.C. — Price 20 cents

LETTER OF TRANSMITTAL

The Honorable, The President of the United States.
The Honorable, The President of the Senate.
The Honorable, The Speaker of the House of Representatives.

I have the honor of transmitting to you the eighth, and final, Annual Report of the Federal Civil Defense Administration. This report is submitted in conformity with section 406, Public Law 920, of the 81st Congress.

Respectfully,

LEO A. HOEGH, *Director*.

PREFACE

This report, which covers the period from July 1, 1957, to June 30, 1958, is the final annual report of the Federal Civil Defense Administration.

On July 1, 1958, FCDA and the Office of Defense Mobilization were merged in a new Agency, the Office of Defense and Civilian Mobilization, a part of the Executive Office of the President. The title of the new Agency was later changed to Office of Civil and Defense Mobilization.

By Executive order, FCDA coordinated Federal assistance in major disasters under the Federal Disaster Act (Public Law 875, 81st Cong.). Agency activities in this program are reflected in a separate report to the Congress.

Chapter 1

PLANNING

In civil as in military defense all activities support the operational plan—the blueprint for action. In 1958, after seven years during which changes in weapons and defensive concepts hampered civil defense operational planning, the plans began to come off the drafting boards.

A National Plan was developed. Basic State and local plans were nearing completion. And because planning is never actually ended, tests to improve the plans continued.

NATIONAL PLAN

One of the first steps taken by Mr. Hoegh when he became Administrator of the Federal Civil Defense Administration on July 19, 1957, was to start work on a National Plan for Civil Defense. After months of intensive work by many people, the basic Plan was completed in the spring of 1958.

For the Plan to reach that stage required the advice and guidance of a number of groups, and coordination not only within the Federal Government but also with State and local governments. For example, the presidentially appointed Civil Defense Advisory Council spent a great deal of time on a detailed review of the Plan. The Medical Advisory Committee, Labor Advisory Committee, and the National Advisory Council on Rural Civil Defense all influenced the Plan's development. The Civil Defense Coordinating Board, which included representatives of all major Federal agencies, met five times for a word-by-word review of the Plan. The executive committees of the National Association of State and Local Civil Defense Directors and the Governors' Conference were among the organizations consulted. Administrator Hoegh personally briefed the President and the Cabinet on the Plan.

All of these groups, and others, were working toward a single objective—a simple but complete statement of the responsibilities and courses of action of the Federal Government, State and local governments, and the individual citizen for carrying out the civil defense mission in the United States. The mission: To protect life and property from the effects of attack by preparing for and by carrying out emergency functions to prevent, minimize, and repair injury and damage.

Although the basic Plan was completed in the spring, it was not distributed immediately. The pending merger of the Federal Civil Defense Administration and the Office of Defense Mobilization

ALWAYS FOLLOW THESE OFFICIAL CIVIL DEFENSE

AIR RAID INSTRUCTIONS

IF ATTACK COMES WITH ↓ NO WARNING	BE QUICK BUT CALM	IF YOU HAVE WARNING ↓
Drop to floor. Try to get under a bed or heavy table.	AT HOME	Turn off stove burners. Go to shelter room you have prepared.
Drop to floor and try to get under desk or bench.	AT WORK	Go to assigned shelter, follow warden's orders.
Drop to floor and bury face in arms. Get out of line with windows.	IN SCHOOL	Go to assigned shelter, follow teacher's orders.
Drop to ground. If cover is close by, dive for it. Bury face in arms.	IN THE OPEN	Get in nearest approved building or shelter, obey CD wardens.
Drop to floor and bury face in arms.	STOP CARS, BUSSES OR TROLLEYS	Get out and go to nearest approved building or shelter, obey CD wardens.

OBEY INSTRUCTIONS AND
STAY PUT UNTIL THE ALL-CLEAR SOUNDS

Read "SURVIVAL UNDER ATOMIC ATTACK," the official U. S. Government booklet. Send 10 cents to the Superintendent of Documents, Government Printing Office, Washington 25, D. C.

GET ONE OF THESE FOR EVERYONE IN YOUR HOME

Civil Defense Air Raid card 1950s. *Utah State Historical Society*

10

required that the Plan be expanded to reflect resource mobilization for nonmilitary defense.[1]

From its inception the National Plan was keyed to the principle that the Federal Government is responsible for the overall direction and coordination of civil defense action. Yet, the Federal Civil Defense Act of 1950 specifically stated that the "responsibility for civil defense shall be vested primarily in the several States and their political subdivisions." A change in the basic law was needed to make the National Plan effective.

The change came in the form of H. R. 7576, introduced in May 1957 by Representative Carl T. Durham (Sixth District, North Carolina). His bill resulted from hearings on Administration-sponsored legislation which was transmitted to the Congress in February 1956 and introduced as H. R. 4910 and H. R. 4911, 85th Congress. H. R. 7576 proposed that "the responsibility for civil defense shall be vested jointly in the Federal Government and the several States and their political subdivisions." Also under the terms of the bill the Federal Government, for the first time, would be allowed to help pay essential personnel and administrative costs of State and local civil defense organizations.

Supporters of the bill saw it as a major factor in promoting unified civil defense planning and action.[2]

STATE AND LOCAL PLANS

While the Federal Government worked on a National Plan, States and localities continued to develop operational plans under the federally financed Survival Projects Program, which was started in 1955 with an initial appropriation of $10 million.

Under the program, 45 States, 3 Territories, and 173 metropolitan areas were conducting studies leading to the development of detailed operational plans.

At the end of the fiscal year, 26 States and one Territory had basic operational plans which were approved by FCDA. They were Alabama, Arkansas, Colorado, Connecticut, Florida, Georgia, Illinois, Kansas, Kentucky, Maine, Massachusetts, Minnesota, Mississippi, Nebraska, New Hampshire, North Carolina, North Dakota, Ohio, Oklahoma,

---

[1] The merger of FCDA and ODM into a new Agency, the Office of Defense and Civilian Mobilization, a part of the Executive Office of the President, took effect on July 1, 1958. The Agency title was later changed to Office of Civil and Defense Mobilization (Public Law 85–763, August 26, 1958). A later draft of the Plan entitled "The National Plan for Civil Defense and Defense Mobilization" was scheduled for distribution early in FY–1959.

[2] The bill became Public Law 85–606, signed by the President on August 8, 1958.

Oregon, Puerto Rico, Rhode Island, South Dakota, Tennessee, Utah, Vermont, and West Virginia.

Most of the plans are expected to be completed during the next fiscal year, but operational planning at the State and local level will continue long after the basic plans are developed.

One important offshoot of the Survival Projects Program was the development of small but competent staffs for State and local civil defense operational planning. Throughout the Nation more than 1,000 persons have been working on State and local civil defense operational plans under the program.

TESTS AND EXERCISES

Among the tests and exercises held during the year was Sentinel II, a "command post" exercise at FCDA Headquarters in December 1957. Civil defense directors of 7 States, 7 cities, and representatives of 20 Federal agencies worked on a simulated problem of formulating actions to insure an adequate food supply for the Nation following a nuclear attack.

Operation Alert 1957 and Phase I (the "attack" phase) of Operation Alert 1958 were conducted during the fiscal year. Many States and cities used the exercises to test and improve civil defense operational plans developed under the Survival Project.

The exercises showed that:

1. More State and local governments are accepting responsibilities to prepare for the emergency of nuclear attack.
2. More Federal agency field offices understand their role in emergency operations.
3. An urgent need exists for effective defense against radioactive fallout.

One important result of the exercises was a plan to expand the Agency's medical stockpile system by the development of a 10-year medical stockpile program. In addition, a growing concern for the serious health and medical care problems that would result from a nuclear attack led to the recommendation that the responsibility for developing civil defense health and medical care plans be assigned to the Department of Health, Education, and Welfare.

The exercises also showed the need for accelerated emergency resource mobilization planning in other fields—manpower, food, fuel, transportation, to name a few. It was probably this factor more than any other that most clearly demonstrated the need for the merger of FCDA and ODM into an Agency within the Executive Office of the President.

Nuclear Attack Plans for Dummies

The operational documents and brochures developed by "small but competent staffs" at the state level often featured tips to minimize panic, such as "drop to the floor," "roll up your car windows," and "wear a wide-brim hat to avoid radiation burns." The Federal Civil Defense Administration's "CD" logo on the cover of the handouts was the government's "stamp of approval." Former North Dakota Lieutenant Governor Lloyd Omdahl eulogized the once-ubiquitous CD logo for the *Bismarck Tribune* after it was discontinued on November 30, 2006.

> According to Omdahl, the first task of the North Dakota Civil Defense Survival Project was to identify sites that would be likely targets in an attack. It was decided that the Minot and Grand Forks Air Force bases would be prime targets because Russia would certainly want to destroy our capacity to retaliate. These selections created consternation in Bismarck and Fargo. They thought they were important enough to be bombed as any other city in North Dakota. From a strategic view, they had no case. However, from a political standpoint, there was no resisting the Bismarck-Fargo axis that has controlled the state since the 1889 constitutional convention. So we committed our Munich and added them to the grand plan, just to win peace in our time.

As Lawrence Freedman wrote in Foreign Affairs that same month, "All governments found it difficult to explain why large amounts of money should be spent on a hopeless contingency."

If the nineteen states and two territories that were tardy on their operational plans in 1958 had been as realistic and to-the-point as Omdahl, they might have avoided the "I" for "incomplete" on their government-issued report cards, while saving paper and money in the process. In his *Bismarck Tribune* article, Omdahl concluded, "Our principal strategy in planning for an enemy attack can be summed up in one word: Run."

CONTINUITY OF GOVERNMENT

One of the top priority programs in the Agency during the year was aimed at preserving and strengthening civil leadership in the event of nuclear attack.

The program was entitled Continuity of Government. Potential audience: more than 100,000 governmental units in the United States—units that form the keystone of civil defense.

The program was based on the premise that civil defense is the inherent responsibility of Federal, State, and local governments, and that civil defense planning should increase the ability of governments to carry out their emergency responsibilities.

Developed with the assistance and advice of hundreds of State and local officials and governmental organizations, the program was first announced by the Administrator at the annual meeting of the United States Civil Defense Council in Detroit on September 5, 1957.[1] The major objectives:

1. Establish emergency lines of succession for top executives, legislators, the judiciary, and other key personnel.
2. Preserve essential records.
3. Establish emergency locations for government operations.
4. Make full use of all governmental, personnel, facilities, and equipment for emergency operations.

A Continuity of Government Office was established in the Agency on November 1, 1957, to administer and promote the program.

Agency officials personally discussed the program with 32 governors during the year, particularly emphasizing the need to establish emergency lines of succession within government. Special briefings stressing the need for lines of succession were given the executive secretaries of the governors in Regions 2, 3, 4, and 5. By the end of the year high officials of nearly every State had become familiar with the program, and it had received the support of such organizations as the Governors' Conference, National Association of County Officials, United States Conference of Mayors, American Municipal Association, United States Civil Defense Council, National Association of State and Territorial Civil Defense Directors, and the American Legion.

---

[1] The program was outlined in FCDA Advisory Bulletin No. 216, Continuity of State and Local Government, September 19, 1957.

Threat Level: "Big Red"

In September 2005, when the enemy threat was not the nuclear arsenal of a military superpower but a low-rent terrorist with an explosive shoe and a box of matches, the state of Nebraska was one of many to revisit their original emergency "line of succession" plans.

Nebraska state officials realized they had overlooked a key provision—that all of the state's lawmakers were to choose three to seven alternates to take their places in case of attack. University of Nebraska Regent Charles Wilson of Lincoln was surprised when told about it by a reporter for the *Omaha World Herald*. "They haven't gotten around to telling me about that yet," he admitted. This was a typical reaction by officials throughout the state.

Doane Kiechel, a Nebraska civil defense official, didn't sound amused in testimony she prepared for state lawmakers. "I am neither joking nor exaggerating in saying that what is about to be remarked in the next ten or fifteen minutes may easily prove later to have been the most important thing I ever said in my life." She went on to list several measures required of lawmakers.

"In light of what's happening in the world today, it's timely to take a look at this," Nebraska Secretary of State John Gale told the *World Herald*.

LINES OF SUCCESSION

When surveys showed that State legislation, and in some cases constitutional amendments, would be required to establish emergency lines of succession at the State and local level, FCDA urged each State to set up a legislative committee or other appropriate group to draft the necessary legislation. To assist these committees the Agency worked on sample or "model" legislation and constitutional amendments.

By June 1958, FCDA had completed sample legislation covering lines of succession for the executive and judicial branches of government, and Columbia University had completed, under contract with FCDA, sample constitutional amendments for all three branches of government.[2] This material was scheduled to be submitted to the Committee on Suggested State Legislation of the Council of State Governments early in fiscal year 1959. If approved by the Committee and the Council, it will be included in the Council's "Recommended State Legislation."

By the end of the year official studies on establishing emergency lines of succession were under way in more than 30 States.

PRESERVING ESSENTIAL RECORDS

A preliminary draft of a manual on preserving essential State and local government records was written for FCDA by an archivist of the National Archives and Records Services. The draft, developed in consultation with State and local government officials, was under review at the end of the year.

EMERGENCY LOCATIONS FOR GOVERNMENT

The Agency obligated more than $2.5 million in Federal matching funds during the fiscal year for the construction of control centers (emergency operations centers) in California, Massachusetts, and Illinois. However, relatively few State and local governments have control centers that could withstand the probable effects of a nuclear attack. Construction cost is a major factor. To help alleviate the situation, the Agency, at the close of the fiscal year, was revising its criteria for approving Federal matching funds for control center construction. For example, immediate costs to State and local governments were to be reduced by permitting construction to be phased over several fiscal periods, and by permitting a maximum calculated risk in the

---

[2]Columbia University (Columbia University Legislative Drafting Research Fund) also was under contract with the Agency to provide early in FY–1959 sample legislation on lines of succession for State and local legislatures.

design of the protective construction required. In addition, the Agency encouraged States and localities to incorporate control centers in new city halls, State office buildings, and other similar buildings.

USING GOVERNMENT PERSONNEL, FACILITIES

The Agency urged State and local governments to make full use of government personnel, facilities, and equipment in emergency operations, and to enroll and train volunteers as auxiliaries to existing government departments. Survival plans were being evaluated on the basis of the application of this principle.

At the Federal level, the delegation of civil defense responsibilities to other Federal agencies is a part of the plan to make full use of government personnel and facilities. No funds were appropriated by the Congress for the delegations program in FY–1958, but prior to that time 5 delegations had been made to 7 Federal agencies.

Chapter 3

RADIOLOGICAL DEFENSE

Fallout, a silent weapon that would endanger every part of the country after a nuclear attack, received increased attention by the Agency in another priority program—Radiological Defense. The program was made up of a number of parts—operational planning, shelter, instrumentation, monitoring, training, public information, and research.

PLANNING

A radiological defense plan was developed as an annex to the National Plan for Civil Defense.[1] The plan assigned radiological defense responsibilities to Federal, State, and local governments, and provided the guidelines for the development of State and local radiological defense plans. Additional guidelines were developed through a New England study for the Agency by Technical Operations, Incorporated, of Burlington, Mass. The study resulted in a draft manual, Radiological Defense Planning Guide, which was under review by the Agency at the end of the year.

---

[1] Later title:The National Plan for Civil Defense and Defense Mobilization (see ch. 1, Planning).

SHELTER

A 5-point National Policy on Shelters was announced by the Administrator on May 7, 1958. The policy, which directly supported the Radiological Defense Program, placed joint responsibility for fallout protection on the Federal Government and the American people. The policy was based on the recognition that, in the event of nuclear attack, "fallout shelters offer the best single nonmilitary defense measure for the protection of the greatest number of our people."

The text of the policy statement follows:

The Administration has conducted exhaustive studies and tests with respect to protective measures to safeguard our citizens against the effects of nuclear weapons. These several analyses have indicated that there is a great potential for the saving of life by fallout shelters. In the event of nuclear attack on this country, fallout shelters offer the best single nonmilitary defense measure for the protection of the greatest number of our people.

Furthermore, a nation with adequate fallout protection is a nation which would be more difficult to successfully attack. This fact alone would substantially lessen the temptation of an aggressor to launch an attack.

The Administration's national civil defense policy, which now includes planning for the movement of people from target areas if time permits, will now also include the use of shelters to provide protection from radioactive fallout.

To implement this established policy, the Administration will undertake the following action:

1. **The Administration will bring to every American all of the facts as to the possible effects of nuclear attack, and inform him of the steps which he and his State and local governments can take to minimize such effects.**
   The present civil defense programs for information and education will therefore be substantially expanded in order to acquaint the people with the fallout hazard and how to effectively overcome it. The public education program will include information on:
   (a) Nuclear weapons effects on people, plants, and animals;
   (b) The provision of effective fallout protection, how to construct a fallout shelter, and how to improvise effective shelter;
   (c) Necessary measures for the protection of food and water;
   (d) How to carry out radiological decontamination; and
   (e) What governments—Federal, State, and local—are themselves doing about fallout protection.

2. **The Administration will initiate a survey of existing structures on a sampling basis, in order to assemble definite information on the capabilities of existing structures to provide fallout shelter, particularly in larger cities.**

Many facilities such as existing buildings, mines, subways, tunnels, cyclone cellars, etc., already afford some fallout protection. Action will be taken to accurately determine the protection afforded by all such facilities in order to make maximum use of them.

3. **The Administration will accelerate research in order to show how fallout shelters may be incorporated in existing, as well as in new, buildings**—whether in homes, other private buildings, or governmental structures. Designs of shelters will be perfected to assure the most economic and effective types.

4. **The Administration will construct a limited number of prototype shelters of various kinds, suitable to different geographical and climatic areas.**

   These will be tested by actual occupancy by differing numbers of people for realistic periods of time. They will also have practical peacetime uses. Some of the prototype structures will be incorporated in:

   (a) Underground parking garages.

   (b) Understreet shelters.

   (c) Subways.

   (d) The Federal highway program—patrol and maintenance facilities.

   (e) Additions to existing schools and new schools, including such facilities as cafeterias, assembly space, and classrooms.

   (f) Additions to existing hospitals and new hospitals, including such facilities as cafeterias, visitors' and convalescent rooms, and reserve areas.

   (g) Industrial plants.

   (h) Commercial buildings.

   (i) Family residences and apartments, including such facilities as bathrooms, garages, basements, and recreation rooms.

5. **The Administration will provide leadership and example by incorporating fallout shelters in appropriate new Federal buildings hereafter designed for civilian use.**

   Federal example is an indispensable element to stimulate State, local government, and private investment for fallout shelters. Community use of shelters in these new buildings is contemplated.

There will be no massive federally financed shelter construction program.

With reference to blast shelters there are still difficult questions having to do with the amount of time that would be available to enter the shelters, the uncertainty of missile accuracy, and the effectiveness of our active defense. There is no assurance that even the deepest shelter would give protection to a sufficient number of people to justify the cost. In addition, there may not be sufficient warning time in view of the development of missile capabilities to permit the effective use of blast shelters.

Our chief deterrent to war will continue to be our active military capability. Our active military defense may eventually have the capability of effectively preventing an enemy from striking intended targets. Highest priority is to be given to the development of this capability.

Common prudence requires that the Federal Government take steps to assist each American to prepare himself—as he would through insurance—against any disaster to meet a possible—although unwanted—eventuality. The national shelter policy is founded upon this principle.

This approach will provide the stimulation necessary for the American people to make preparations for fallout protection. The Federal Government will also work with State and local governments and with private industries to expedite and facilitate the provision of fallout shelter.

The Administration believes that when the American people fully understand the problem that confronts them, they will rise to meet the challenge, as they have invariably done in the past. This is particularly true now that the national policy has been declared, backed up with Federal example, Federal leadership, and Federal guidance. The President has directed me to put this policy into effect.

Protection of our people is not new in the United States. When a free America was being built by our forebears, every log cabin and every dwelling had a dual purpose—namely, a home and a fortress. Today, the citizen should be called upon to make the same contribution as our forebears not for building a free America, but for sustaining a free America.

INSTRUMENTATION

The Agency more than doubled the number of radiological instruments distributed to States and Territories for training and operational preparedness. By the end of the year more than 76,000 instruments had been distributed to States and Territories as compared with 35,000 at the end of FY–1957. The total included more than 40,000 survey meters, 24,000 dosimeters, and 11,000 dosimeter chargers.

In addition, more than 300,000 instruments were stored in Agency warehouses for rapid distribution in the event of a national emergency, and the Agency loaned or transferred nearly 50,000 instruments to 14 other Federal agencies to improve the operational readiness of the Federal Government.

A growing problem in instrument maintenance was eased with the start of a new maintenance program, and the assignment of maintenance technicians to 11 warehouses used, by the Agency for instrument storage.

Two Weeks in Grandma's Pantry

According to a report published in 1962 by the National Academy of Sciences called "Behavioral Science and Civil Defense," "Control Centers like the one located in a hillside near Portland, Oregon, with its 26-inch concrete roof, are being built in various parts of the country. This center can house 300 people for two weeks. It has its own electric and sanitation systems as well as food and water supply." The report also describes another control center in DuPage County, Illinois, that "can withstand a blast pressure over and above existing atmospheric pressure of thirty pounds per square inch . . . and can house 60 people for two weeks."

The idea appears frequently in educational training films and brochures that fallout survivability would need to be about two weeks before the expected "all clear" signal from CONELRAD radio. This apparently had less to do with the fallout threat than with research on how long family members could stand to be cooped up with each other in tight quarters before extremes in human behavior started revealing themselves. No one wants to see Granny devoured by Uncle Earl, regardless of the radioactive consequences.

Believe it or not, the Civil Defense mandate to stock food and supplies for two weeks had the comforting name of "Grandma's Pantry." The message was well-received by American industry and commerce, including Kraft, a company that was more than happy to supply our grandmothers with such self-sufficient delicacies as Minute Rice (created in 1949), Cheez Whiz (1950), and Tang (1957, well ahead of the Apollo program that really popularized it), and Sears Roebuck, which set up five hundred Grandma's Pantry exhibits throughout its department store chain. Was it altruism, commercial exploitation, or both? Whatever the reason, what could be more American (and patriotic) than to help Grandma stock her pantry against the Soviet threat?

MONITORING

A program was started to establish a Federal network of radiological monitoring stations which could provide hourly reports on the level of fallout radiation across the Nation after a nuclear attack. The network will be composed of existing Federal personnel and facilities. Initial aim of the program is to establish radiological monitoring stations at 700 fixed field facilities of the United States Weather Bureau and the Civil Aeronautics Administration. During FY–1958 those two agencies began equipping their field facilities with radiological survey instruments and training field personnel to use the instruments.

The Agency plans to expand this network by using the personnel and facilities of other Federal agencies. The aim is to have at least one Federal monitoring station in each of the more than 3,000 counties in the United States.

In addition, the Agency expanded its radiological instrument (see above) and training programs (see below, and ch. 5, Training and Information) to assist States and localities in preparing for radiological monitoring.

TRAINING, INFORMATION, AND RESEARCH

As the result of Agency training programs some 2,500 instructors in radiological monitoring and 75,000 radiological meter readers had been trained by the end of the year.

In addition, a radiological defense high school program was developed in cooperation with the Office of Education, departments of education in the States, and State civil defense directors to:

1. Help high schools incorporate radiological defense education into their science courses, and
2. Improve the geographical distribution of radiation detection instruments.[2]

Scheduled to start early in FY–1959, the program will include the distribution of a specially designed radiological instrument kit to 15,000 high schools throughout the United States. The kit consists of 4 survey meters, 4 dosimeters, 1 dosimeter charger, 2 containers of a low-intensity radiation source, batteries, and an instruction manual on using the instruments.

The Agency carried out expanded public information and research programs in radiological defense. Additional information on radiological training and public information activities may be found in Chapter 5, Training and Information. For information on radiological research see Chapter 6, Research.

---

[2] The high school program is *not* an attempt to train teen-age radiological monitors for duty during a national emergency.

Chapter 4

EMERGENCY SYSTEMS AND EQUIPMENT

Adequate civil defense preparations cannot be made with money and hardware alone. Dedicated people are needed. But those who do the job must have tools—good tools.

In FY–1958 more tools were made available to them. No one would argue that the amount was sufficient, but significant progress was made.

This "hardware" section of the Annual Report describes progress in the warning, communications, stockpiling, Federal contributions, and surplus property programs.

WARNING

Seventy-six warning points were added to the National Warning System during the year, raising the total number of warning points across the Nation to 276. Plans were being made to expand this network to 500 warning points as part of the groundwork for faster and more direct warning of enemy attack.

At the end of the year the network consisted of 4 FCDA Warning Centers at major Air Force installations,[1] 49 State Warning Points (including Washington, D.C.), and 227 other warning points. The network was capable of sending a warning to all 276 warning points in about 15 seconds.[2]

This network is tied to the many outdoor warning systems (usually siren systems) installed by municipalities to warn the public of an enemy attack.[3] A total of 134 cities are considered to have virtually complete coverage with their outdoor warning systems. However, there is still a problem of warning people in their homes or other buildings where the outdoor devices may not be heard. Research was continued during the year to develop internal warning systems by making use of existing power lines or telephone facilities.

---

[1] FCDA National Warning Center at North American Air Defense Command Headquarters, Colorado Springs, Colo.; FCDA Eastern Warning Center at Headquarters, Eastern NORAD Region, Stewart Air Force Base, N. Y.; FCDA Central Warning Center at Headquarters, Central NORAD Region, Richards-Gebaur Air Force Base, Mo.; FCDA Western Warning Center at Headquarters, Western NORAD Region, Hamilton Air Force Base, Calif.

[2] The Federal Government pays all communications costs of the network, but States and localities supply the personnel for the 276 warning points.

[3] The Federal Government pays half the cost of installing and maintaining municipal outdoor warning systems.

Work continued on the installation of a special warning network in the Washington, D.C., metropolitan area. A system of sirens, scheduled to be completely installed in fiscal year 1960, will be capable of covering an area within a 20-mile radius of the center of the District. Alternate facilities will permit control of the sirens by each political subdivision within the area or from a classified location outside the area.

COMMUNICATIONS

The primary system of operational communications for the Agency is National Communications System No. 1 (NACOM 1). It consists of about 20,000 miles of leased wire facilities—private line telephone and teletypewriter services—connecting the Agency's Battle Creek office (Lowpoint) with a classified location outside of Washington, with the Agency's Regional Offices, and State civil defense offices.

The circuits of NACOM 1 can be used for both telephone (voice) or teletypewriter communication. The principal purpose of the system, however, is to provide a record communications media. Therefore the circuits are used primarily for teletypewriter communication.

During the fiscal year the circuits were improved between Lowpoint and the classified location. The speed of transmission was increased from 60 words a minute to 75 words a minute. In addition, special equipment was installed at the Regional Offices for handling classified messages. The equipment is similar to that previously installed at Lowpoint and the classified location.

Preliminary design work was completed on a system of radio backup to NACOM 1. This radio network, scheduled for installation in FY–1959, will be called NACOM 2 and will provide for 2-way radio communication between the Agency's Battle Creek office, Regional Offices, and the classified location. Extension of NACOM to the State level is planned for fiscal years 1960 and 1961.

At the State and local level, the Radio Amateur Emergency Services (RACES) program continued to expand. About 1,000 State, area, county, and city RACES operational plans were approved by the end of the year. Only two States did not have RACES plans, but several localities in each of these States did have accepted plans. All Regional Headquarters of the Agency had radio equipment in use at the start of the year for contact with State RACES networks, and additional equipment was authorized during the year to improve this system.

STOCKPILING

The Agency collected and analyzed a considerable amount of data to determine the feasibility, amount, and cost of stockpiling essential emergency items in the major categories of medical equipment and

And the Hoboes Will Rule the Earth

According to "Behavioral Science and Civil Defense," a report by the National Academy of Sciences (1962), "Assurance that the public will respond satisfactorily to the warning signals is another matter. The manner in which people might respond to the warning signals of an actual attack has been the subject of research in three accidental or false alerts."

The research focused on the reasons for failure to properly heed warnings: "Those who are too strongly bound by the old norms of regulating means, or who are incapable of successfully engaging in innovative behavior . . . may abandon the goal [of successful casualty reduction] but keep up the activities originally intended to achieve it—ritualistic behavior. Or the frustrated may give up on both ends and means and engage in retreatism—become drunks, hoboes, drug addicts, or mentally ill."

One would imagine that *hoboes* is no longer the government-sanctioned term.

supplies, food, and engineering supplies for different types of attack conditions. The effect that the Nation's transportation system would have on the location of emergency supplies was one of the important segments of the study which will provide the basic information needed for a long-range expansion of the Agency's stockpiling program.

Although no money was appropriated to purchase additional stockpile items in FY–1958, a little over $3 million was appropriated to store and maintain existing stocks.

As part of the maintenance program certain antibiotics and vaccines that were about to become outdated were replaced from manufacturers' stocks at a fraction of their original cost. In addition, 32,807 units of outdated plasma were reworked by various contractors into serum albumin at about 25 percent of the original cost.

The Agency established 10 stockpile maintenance service shops and 11 radiological maintenance service shops at its warehouses to maintain emergency hospital equipment and radiological defense instruments.

At the end of the year the Agency had stockpiled medical and radiological defense items valued at about $200 million and engineering items (including generators, chlorinators, water purifiers, pumps, and pipe) valued at about $7 million.

The breakdown for major medical and radiological defense items was as follows: 932 emergency civil defense hospital units;[4] 10,317,500 burn dressings; 3,187,000 blood recipient sets; 1,580,000 units of blood derivatives (plasma and serum albumin); 4,550,000 units of plasma expanders; 32,500 gas masks; 6,188,000 doses of atropine; 57,571,000 doses of vaccines and antitoxins (part in manufacturers' storage); 1,584,000 paper blankets; 308,000 litters; 238,000 radiological dosimeters; and 159,000 radiological survey meters.[5]

FEDERAL CONTRIBUTIONS

Federal matching funds contributed to States, Territories, and possessions for civil defense programs amounted to 46 cents per capita in FY–1958 as compared with 38 cents per capita in 1957—an increase of more than 20 percent.

From the start of the program in FY–1952 through FY–1958 more than $80 million in matching funds has been contributed by the Federal Government. At least an equal amount has been spent

---

[4] Stored in FCDA, State, and local sites. In addition, about 93 percent of the material for an additional 1,000 emergency hospital units had been delivered and assembly started.

[5] Includes instruments on loan or grant to States.

The Return of the Dosimeters

Dosimeters and other relics of the Cold War era had their day again in the post-9/11 era. About a month after the September 11 attacks, Robert Byers of the *Charleston Gazette* wrote that "the American Civil Defense Association is offering its usual fare of dosimeters, water filtration systems, and potassium iodide tablets ($16.95 a bottle for association members), which fill up your thyroid and block it from accepting radioactive iodine in the case of a radiation emergency."

In 2003, *Florida Today* columnist Jeff Schweers described websites that "offer everything from free plans for building your own shelter to custom installation jobs costing upward of $70,000" in addition to "military-style ready-to-eat meals, civil defense radiation detection survey meters, Geiger counters and dosimeters, . . . plans and training material," and other such literature, courtesy of your local FEMA office, the FCDA's modern successor in emergency affairs.

Dosimeters provide individual radiation exposure information for the Radioactive Citizen. Worn clipped to a pocket or belt, the user merely had to look through the eyepiece (the black end) while pointing the dosimeter at a light source—like using a View-Master!—to see a roentgens scale indicating exposure levels.

by States and localities.

In the early years of the program Federal contributions were used primarily for health and special weapons defense items. Recently, however, States and localities have used most of the money to buy communications equipment. The trend was continued in 1958 with about 54 percent of the contributions money being used to buy communications equipment.

From the start of the program through FY–1958, about 70 percent of the contributions went to States in the east and west—Regions 1, 2, and 7.

SURPLUS PROPERTY

Since 1957, when Congress authorized making Federal surplus property available to States for civil defense purposes, surplus equipment originally costing more than $35.6 million has been donated for this purpose. Most of the total ($31 million) was donated in FY–1958.

Motor vehicles and trailers, electrical equipment, fire fighting and rescue equipment, construction and excavating equipment, communications equipment, tractors, engines, and hand tools made up more than 70 percent of the surplus equipment donated to States under the program.

Chapter 5

TRAINING AND INFORMATION

The best planning, research, and operational equipment will fall short of providing an adequate civil defense unless people understand what has to be done and are trained to do their part of the job. The Agency's training and public information programs during the year were aimed at strengthening this vital link in civil defense preparedness.

TRAINING

Agency instructors conducted 43 training courses during the year which were attended by 1,163 persons. This raised to 15,550 the total number of persons who have received instruction in Agency training schools.

Four schools were operated: the Staff College, oldest school of the Agency; the Radiological Defense School; the Rescue Instructor

Training Center;[1] and a newly established Eastern Instructor Training Center at Brooklyn, N.Y.

Emphasis was given to radiological defense training. More than 400 persons attended 15 courses presented by the Radiological Defense School at Battle Creek, in each Agency Region, and at the new Eastern Instructor Training Center. The school's most frequently given course was "Radiological Monitoring for Instructors," which was given 12 times to a total of 377 persons. The course is designed to train Federal, State, and local instructors who will train others in radiological defense monitoring. Other courses given by the school were the "Radiological Defense Officer" course, "Radiological Aspects of Nonmilitary Defense," and "Radiological Instrument Operation."

The Staff College gave 8 courses to a total of 263 persons. The courses were "Elements of Nonmilitary Defense for State and Local Officials," given three times; "State and Local Action in Natural Disasters," given twice; and "Emergency Management and Operations for State and Local Officials," "Emergency Management and Operations for County Officials," and "Federal Action in Major Disasters," each given once.

Although most Staff College instruction is done at Battle Creek, Mich., some courses are given by a traveling team. In 1958, two courses, "Elements of Nonmilitary Defense for State and Local Officials" and "Local Action in Natural Disasters," were given to a total of 55 persons in Arkansas. In addition, 9 States gave 16 civil defense courses to a total of 772 persons as a result of contracts made with the Staff College.

The new Eastern Instructor Training Center was opened on June 9, 1958.[2] The center will be used to train instructors who will return home and train others in the procedures and skills required for effective emergency operations. Plans were made during the year to open a similar center in the west.

The Nation's school systems are a major resource available to advance the concepts of civil defense, and the Agency worked with the United States Office of Education and recognized national education organizations to make use of this resource. For example, as the result of a Civil Defense Education Project in the United States Office of Education, lectures on aspects of radiological defense were given at 55 seminars attended by some 3,000 high school science teachers during fiscal years 1957 and 1958.[3] Also, the Office of Education prepared a manual for the Agency, *Nuclear Science Teaching Aids and Activities*,

---

[1] The Rescue Instructor Training School at Olney, Md., was closed at the end of the fiscal year, but rescue training was scheduled as part of the curriculum at the Eastern Instructor Training Center.

[2] The first course, "Radiological Monitoring for Instructors," was attended by 29 persons.

[3] The seminars are sponsored annually by the National Science Foundation and are held during the summer months.

which was scheduled for publication in FY–1959 and distribution to high school science teachers, particularly those participating in the Agency's new radiological defense high school program (see ch. 3, Radiological Defense). Cooperating with the Agency, the Adult Education Association and the National School Boards Association prepared civil defense publications, making a total of 5 publications developed to describe the civil defense responsibilities of specific educational groups. Some 150,000 copies of the new publications, *Civil Defense for Adult Americans* and *School Boards Plan for Disaster Problems*, were distributed. In addition, a contract was made with the American Association of School Administrators to have that organization prepare a civil defense support publication in FY–1959. Another contract was negotiated with the George Peabody College for Teachers, Nashville, Tenn., to develop civil defense curriculum materials for use by teacher training institutions throughout the Nation.

INFORMATION

The Agency produced 30 new publications, 3 motion pictures, 11 television and radio station break announcements, 69 magazine articles, and 91 news releases as part of its public information program.

The most popular single item of public information was a wallet-size Civil Defense Preparedness card, which describes the attack warning signals and the main actions families should take to prepare themselves for a possible enemy attack.

As a direct result of a brief mention of this card by the Administrator on the Dave Garroway television show in March 1958, thousands of requests were made for it. By the end of the fiscal year more than 25 million cards had been distributed throughout the Nation.

The wallet card and 4 other publications accounted for more than 36 million copies of publications distributed by the Agency during the year. The others: *Operation Survival*, an illustrated booklet for school children (4 million copies distributed), *Facts About Fallout Protection*, a public leaflet (more than 3.7 million copies), *Family Shelters Against Radioactive Fallout*, a technical bulletin (more than 1.8 million copies), and *Home Protection Exercises*, a public booklet (more than 1.7 million copies).

In addition, the Agency developed a *Handbook for Emergencies*, which was scheduled to be distributed by the Boy Scouts of America on October 11, 1958, to more than 40 million homes.

More than 3.5 million persons saw civil defense exhibits prepared by the Agency. The exhibits were displayed 94 different times at National, State, and local civil defense meetings; industrial

WHEN THE WARNING SOUNDS

A STEADY BLAST OF 3 TO 5 MINUTES

This means: **ATTACK ALERT—TAKE ACTION AS DIRECTED BY LOCAL GOVERNMENT.**

Tune your AM radio to a **Conelrad** frequency **(640 or 1240)** for official directions. Proceed according to your community's emergency action plan. **Don't use the telephone.**

WAILING TONE OR SHORT BLASTS FOR 3 MINUTES

This means: **ATTACK—TAKE COVER IMMEDIATELY IN BEST AVAILABLE SHELTER.**

In a building: If there is no prepared shelter, go into a basement or to an interior first floor room. Stay in shelter until you get word you can leave.

Outdoors or in a car: Go to nearest shelter. If you cannot reach prepared shelter lie flat on the ground face down, or crouch on floor of car.

CIVIL DEFENSE PREPAREDNESS

PREPARE:

Your family shelter and equip with two-week supply of food and water, first aid kit, battery radio.

Evacuation kit for your automobile with food, water, first aid kit, battery or car radio, blankets.

LEARN:

1. Warning signals and what they mean.
2. Your community plan for emergency action.
3. Protection from radioactive fallout.
4. First aid and home emergency preparedness.
5. Use of **CONELRAD—640 or 1240** for official directions.

Civil Defense Preparedness Card (front and back).
United States Government Printing Office

conferences; meetings of educational organizations; and State and county fairs.

At the end of the year the Agency's public information program was pointed toward implementing the National Policy on Shelters (see ch. 3, Radiological Defense) and the self-help aspects of the pending National Plan for Civil Defense and Defense Mobilization (see ch. 1, Planning).

Chapter 6

RESEARCH

Agency research is primarily applied research directed toward the practical application of science to the problems of civil defense. The Agency obligated nearly $8.5 million for research in FY–1958—an increase of more than 20 percent over the previous fiscal year.

Highlights of the research program in the major categories of radiological defense, shelter studies, warning and communications, health and medical care studies, social and economic research, and operations research, follow:

RADIOLOGICAL DEFENSE

1. *Radiation Physics.*—The National Bureau of Standards made good progress during the year on basic studies of the characteristics of radiation produced by nuclear weapons, the penetrability of radiation in various construction materials and buildings, and methods of protecting the population from penetrating radiation. The results of these studies are used by the Agency and its contractors in developing radiological defense plans.

2. *Shielding Evaluation.*—A study was started by Technical Operations, Inc., of Burlington, Mass., to evaluate radiation shielding provided by large structures. There are five major goals in the study: (a) to obtain, by direct measurement, radiation attenuation provided by one or more large buildings; (b) to compare these measurements with the results of theoretical computations of attenuation; (c) to determine significant geometrical parameters of a building which must be measured to calculate its shielding potential; (d) to identify factors in building construction which could most easily be changed to effect a significant improvement in shielding; and (e) to summarize

Save the Cows!

The conclusion reached after years of government research on the science of radiation can be summed up as follows: nuclear fallout does weird things to the human body . . . and can kill cattle too. Secret documents that were only declassified decades after the 1958 annual report indicate that our bovine friends were of primary concern in this research. Humans and their offspring were a trickier category to pin down, it seems.

Everyone who paid attention to what happened post–Hiroshima and Nagasaki knew there were strange aftereffects associated with fallout, but few American citizens objected to the plan to conduct these tests in Nevada beginning in 1951. Even downwind residents from the test sites supported the government's rationale for official secrecy. National security concerns during the Korean War provided the justification to keep knowledge of the collateral damage from these tests from the public for several decades.

The fears of many baby boomer mothers over their kids catching snowflakes on their tongues during the era of above-ground atomic testing might sound paranoid, but as it turns out, Mother indeed knew best. On August 1, 1994, Los Alamos National Laboratory released previously declassified documents reporting that "blue snow" fell five hundred miles from a 28-kiloton Nevada Test Range blast in 1955, after which reports came in from the area around Eagle Nest, New Mexico, about "cattle suffering from inflamed udders and children [who] were complaining of reddened faces and swollen tongues."

The document goes on to say that "within the next 60 days several cattle died of unknown causes while pasturing in a remote meadow in this area." It did not reveal any attempt to investigate the extent to which children were affected, or any estimate of how many fell ill. After livestock manure, pasture, and soil samples were taken from the area, a health division report gave the official rationale for this omission: "In the interest of good public relations, veterinary assistance would be enlisted to investigate the report more completely."

and develop a detailed procedure for use by engineering contractors in fallout shelter surveys.

Tests at the Nevada Test Site were conducted jointly by the Agency, the Bureau of Standards, the University of California, and the Atomic Energy Commission on the radiation shielding provided by residential structures. Radioactive sources, distributed at 2-foot intervals around and on the roofs of houses that had withstood actual atomic explosions several years ago, were used in conducting the tests. The effectiveness of certain improvised fallout protective measures also was investigated.

3. *Radiological Reclamation.* A study was undertaken for the Agency by the Naval Radiological Defense Laboratory to develop information and criteria as a base for planning and implementing large-scale radiological reclamation operations. One immediate object of the study is determining the feasibility of various large-scale reclamation procedures, including the "cost" in terms of radiation exposure, financial, and logistic factors.

NRDL also started work on the development of a radiological reclamation manual for the Agency which will be comparable to the NRDL manual entitled *Radiological Recovery of Fixed Military Installations.* The manual will contain information on operational procedures in radiological decontamination and other reclamation actions applicable to industrial, residential, and rural areas.

4. *Instruments.*—A prototype of an aerial radiological survey instrument was tested at the AEC Nevada Test Site, and tests of production models of the prototype were scheduled for early in FY–1959.

A transistorized model of the low-range survey meter (CD V–700) was developed during the year, substantially reducing the problem of supplying batteries for survey meters.

Prototypes of a remote monitoring fixed station instrument were developed. Such an instrument will permit a person to read the outside radiation level while remaining in a protected location.

The Jordan Electronics Division of the Victoreen Instrument Co. started work on a transistorized loudspeaker for a Geiger survey meter. The speaker attachment will be used as a teaching aid for classroom instruction.

5. *Operational Planning.*—A continuing research program with the University of California, aimed at providing techniques for use in radiological defense planning, covered the following studies during the year:

    (a) *Shielding.*—The project includes studies of the shielding afforded by large buildings and basements. Initial results indicate that it will be possible to evaluate radiation shielding provided in large, complex buildings by making only a few

New Industry, New Suspicions

The Jordan Electronics Division of the Victoreen Instrument Company was part of an industry officially introduced to the world in the December 1949 issue of the *Bulletin of the Atomic Scientists*:

ANNOUNCEMENT

The birth of the Nucleonic Instruments Industry was signalized in New York November 1 and 2, 1949. Nucleonic manufacturers to the number of 23 or more combined in an Exhibit of their own at the Hotel Commodore in connection with a specialized instrumentation conference with papers by leading scientific authorities, under the auspices of the Institute of Radio Engineers and the American Institute of Electrical Engineers. Steps were taken toward forming a permanent nucleonic group organization.

Nucleonics—a fancy name for instruments used in nuclear research—soon became a multi-billion-dollar industry. Scientists flocked to this new field as universities around the world saw the growth potential and quickly modeled new coursework after the famed Oak Ridge Institute in Tennessee. However, the political and military climate during the growing arms race made it virtually impossible to compare notes across national borders without suspicion.

Academic purists were soon at loggerheads with the U.S. State Department over impediments to scientific travel. In response, the Federation of American Scientists established the Passport Committee in 1951 to foster international scientific cooperation, but suspicion still ran rampant within the field.

In the early 1950s, Manhattan Project physicist Martin David Kamen was accused of being a Communist spy. A House Un-American Activities Committee (HUAC) investigation got him blacklisted. The State Department denied Kamen a passport and the right to travel. In his greatest despair, Kamen attempted suicide.

His fortunes turned in 1955 when he won a libel suit against the *Chicago Tribune.* The newspaper had gone further than HUAC, calling Kamen a "traitor," and ran a photo reportedly showing him with a Russian "who had in his pocket certain secret papers" that Kamen "had transmitted to him." According to Kamen, the Passport Committee took an interest in his case, even raising funds to support it. After winning, one of Kamen's first actions was to obtain a new passport.

physical measurements.

(b) *Radioactive Fallout Contour Maps.*—A method was developed for computing and preparing maps showing contour lines of fallout radiation intensities and doses estimated for various locations on the basis of probable wind patterns and characteristics. Maps were prepared for summer and winter conditions in the San Francisco Bay area, and computations were completed for 11 Western States.

(c) *Variations in Fallout Distribution.*—The influence of topography, surface winds, eddies, and air currents are being studied to determine the drifting characteristics of fallout around buildings in urban communities. Initial results indicate that certain trends can be established. Local decisions on locations for fallout shelters and how to alter existing buildings to provide more fallout protection will be influenced by these studies.

(d) *Effects of Mass Fire on Fallout.*—Nuclear bursts on metropolitan areas are likely to start mass fires resulting in strong ascending columns of air. These columns of air may be sufficient to disperse substantial amounts of fallout away from the area of burst. Research on a laboratory scale is being undertaken jointly with the California Forest and Range Experiment Station to evaluate the deposition of fallout particles in the presence of fire-induced convection columns.

(e) *Effects of Fallout on Water Resources.*—A study is being made of the probable effects of fallout on water resources and supplies. The purpose is to provide information for the radiological decontamination of water supplies. This information will be published in a handbook for water supply personnel.

The United States Weather Bureau expanded on its earlier study of upper wind data to provide the basis for fallout probability charts. The results of the project will be incorporated in radiological defense studies at the University of California.

A study aimed at the development of model State and local radiological defense plans was conducted for the Agency by Technical Operations, Inc., of Burlington, Mass. The study, carried out in the States of New York and New Jersey, resulted in drafts of model plans to minimize the number of radiological casualties from a nuclear attack by making the best possible use of existing resources. A draft manual, *Radiological Defense Planning Guide*, containing the model plans and the data and analyses on which they were based, was being reviewed by the Agency at the end of the fiscal year.

SHELTER STUDIES

1. *Nevada Tests.*—Engineering field tests of structures and equipment were conducted during the first quarter of the fiscal year at the Nevada Test Site. These included tests on reinforced concrete dome structures, dual-purpose concrete mass shelters, family shelters, French and German shelters, protective vaults, thermal activated air-zero locators, pressure-sensitive valves and ventilation equipment, and the behavior of certain shelter doors under blast loadings. Test reports were being prepared at the end of the fiscal year. Plans were made to conduct additional tests to determine the effect of shock in deep underground tunnels.

2. *Prototype Design and Specifications.*—A contract was signed with Eberle M. Smith Associates, Inc., of Detroit, for the design of three dual-purpose fallout shelters for elementary schools.

The Armour Research Foundation of Chicago started a study of the vulnerability of a system of deep rock shelters. (A previous study by another contractor resulted in a preliminary design for a system of deep rock shelters—800 feet belowground—for the daytime population of the Borough of Manhattan.) In the Armour study, a technical review of geological formations and an analysis of the shock effects of surface-burst nuclear weapons will be made to determine the vulnerability of the Manhattan design for deep rock shelters. Other sites, such as Chicago, Pittsburgh, Detroit, Kansas City, Cleveland, and boroughs adjacent to Manhattan, will be investigated to determine the influence that local geology has on the degree of protection offered by deep rock shelters.

3. *Shelter Equipment.*—Eleven valves, designed by Arthur D. Little, Inc., of Cambridge, Mass., for opening and closing ventilating intake and exhaust systems in shelters, were tested at the Nevada Test Site to determine their ability to close quickly and to withstand the shock load from a nuclear blast. The Bureau of Reclamation laboratories in Denver conducted additional tests on the valves to determine the air pressure drop associated with varying rates of airflow through the valves. The aim is to develop valves for shelter ventilating systems that are strong enough to withstand nuclear blast and yet flexible enough for rapid operation.

WARNING AND COMMUNICATIONS

1. *Telephone Warning System.*—A research project was completed on methods for transmitting a warning from a telephone exchange to all subscribers. The system as demonstrated by field tests was not considered economically feasible.

2. *Powerline Warning System.*—The Midwest Research Institute of Kansas City, Mo., is developing a National Emergency Alarm Repeater powerline warning system which can transmit a nationwide warning to users of electric power who have a special warning receiver. At the end of the fiscal year a field test was under way on a large power network to determine the best methods for generating the warning signal. Several prototype warning receivers will be tested to develop a reliable, inexpensive receiver that may be plugged into any ordinary 110-volt alternating current outlet.

3. *Communications.*—Research and preliminary studies were continued by FCDA communications specialists on various types of communications equipment, including a mobile communications center, antenna systems, control center communications systems, radio and television broadcast coverage analysis, and communications equipment for shelters.

HEALTH AND MEDICAL CARE STUDIES

1. *Biological Effects of Nuclear Warfare.*—Studies of the biological effects of blast were conducted by the Lovelace Foundation for Medical Education and Research of Albuquerque, N. Mex., with support by FCDA and AEC.

A continuing study by the United States Naval Radiological Defense Laboratory on biological aspects of nuclear radiation produced interim reports but no basic conclusions. Areas of study include the diagnosis and treatment of radiation injury, internal radiation hazards, biological effects of deeply penetrating radiation, surface effects of radiation, metabolic and pathologic changes produced by radiation, and the determination of individual and species differences in susceptibility to radiation. In addition, NRDL began studies for the Agency of the relationship between acute and late effects of ionizing radiation, and the evaluation and application of therapeutic measures.

2. *Chemical Warfare Defense.*—The Engineering Research and Development Laboratories of the Corps of Engineers started a study to develop procedures for removing nerve gas from water by using the facilities and chemicals available in conventional municipal water treatment plants.

Agreements were reached with the Army Chemical Corps for final engineering tests and completion of procurement documents on a previously designed civilian protective mask (CD V–805), and an infant protector.

3. *Blood Research.*—The Agency participated in a continuing blood research program of the Army Medical Corps. The program includes research on plasma volume expanders and other research relating to

blood and shock therapy. One immediate object of the Agency in this program is the development of additional expanders which can be substituted for whole human blood and plasma.

Another continuing project is being directed by the National Academy of Sciences to find ways of processing whole blood plasma which will eliminate the danger of infecting a plasma recipient with the hepatitis virus. Several commercial laboratories are working with the National Academy of Sciences on this project.

4. *Training.*—The National League for Nursing started a project for the Agency aimed at integrating civil defense and disaster nursing methods in the training programs for registered and practical nurses.

5. *Medical Care Operations.*—The American Medical Association is directing a study for the Agency to develop the planning, training, and operational organization needed as a basis for a National Emergency Medical Care Plan. The AMA Commission on National Emergency Medical Care has appointed three task forces, representing medicine, surgery, dentistry, veterinary medicine, nursing, and public health, to complete the study.

SOCIAL AND ECONOMIC RESEARCH

1. *Human Behavior Under Stress.*—Three studies were completed analyzing human behavior during natural disasters. Dr. Harry E. Moore, professor of sociology at the University of Texas, produced a report entitled *Tornadoes Over Texas—A Study of Waco and San Angela in Disaster* in which he analyzed the social disorganization and the recovery of the two Texas cities following large-scale disasters. The Disaster Research Group of the National Academy of Sciences directed a project for the Agency entitled *A Study of Formal Organizations in Hurricane Audrey*, which evaluated the manner in which formal organizations of Government, the American National Red Cross, and other groups and individuals dealt with disaster conditions. The Disaster Research Group also directed for the Agency a study of the human, social, management, and other factors and problems involved in the stranding of 800 persons in a Pennsylvania Turnpike Restaurant during a March 1958 blizzard.

The Agency and the Disaster Research Group jointly developed a series of major sociopsychological findings on human behavior under disaster and war conditions, and described their applicability to conditions of nuclear warfare.

2. *Public Attitudes.*—The Survey Research Center of the University of Michigan in the latter part of 1957 conducted a survey of the effects of the "Sputnik" launching on public attitudes toward fallout, the imminence of war, and the need for protective measures such as

shelter. The findings were correlated with earlier public opinion and attitude surveys conducted by the Center to produce data on public opinion and attitude change.

3. *Survival Supplies for Civilians.*—The Business and Defense Services Administration of the Department of Commerce started a project in March 1958 which has as its purpose improving the ability of the Federal Government to estimate the requirements for and the availability of certain essential civilian supply items in a national emergency. Various exercises, such as the annual Operation Alert, have demonstrated the inadequacy of this type of information. This project is to correct this inadequacy by surveying the availability of essential survival items, supplying tapes for inclusion in the resources file of the National Damage Assessment Center, and developing techniques for quickly determining the location and quantity of survival items.

4. *Continuity of Government.*—A contract was signed with Columbia University for the development of a model State constitutional amendment which, if adopted, would enable State legislatures to pass laws on lines of succession for essential positions in the executive, legislative, and judicial branches of government.

5. *Training.*—Applied Psychological Services of Villanova University, in a continuing program, evaluated the effectiveness of various Agency training courses and techniques.

OPERATIONS RESEARCH

1. *Damage Assessment.*—The Agency's Damage Assessment System for rapidly estimating damage to people and essential resources following a nuclear attack was improved during the year, and extended to include United States Territories. In addition, the Stanford Research Institute, contractors for the Agency's system, worked on revising the computing program of the system so that it can be used in the high-speed electronic computers at the National Damage Assessment Center. Also, the Bureau of the Census started work to update the resources file used in the system.

2. *Strategic Framework Study.*—The Stanford Research Institute conducted a study of the offensive and defensive capabilities of Russia and the United States so that the civil defense job of this Nation could be seen within an overall offense-defense framework. The study is used by the Agency to develop estimates of how certain civil defense actions could influence the total defensive and retaliatory power of the Nation. An outgrowth of this research project was an analysis, developed for the Federal Government, of the survival of the population after a massive attack in 1965.

Chapter 7

CIVIL DEFENSE PARTICIPATION BY
SPECIAL GROUPS AND ORGANIZATIONS

The Agency worked with a number of groups and organizations in this country and with other friendly countries to improve civil defense during the year. For example, the American Legion developed, under Agency guidance, a light duty rescue training program aimed at training rescue units in each of the more than 17,000 Legion posts and 14,000 Legion auxiliary units. The rescue units will be incorporated as auxiliaries to local fire, police, or public works departments.

This chapter is intended to show the scope of Agency activities with various groups and organizations rather than a detailed report of these activities.

INTERNATIONAL COOPERATION

With the advice and guidance of the Department of State, the Agency took part in five international conferences, exchanged public and technical information with other countries, cooperated in a continuing program of exchange visits of civil defense authorities, and arranged for the participation by other governments in the civil effects test program at the Atomic Energy Commission Nevada Test Site.

1. *North Atlantic Treaty Organization.*—The Administrator took part in the fourth conference of the NATO Senior Civil Emergency Planning Committee, which was established in 1955 to advise the North Atlantic Council on all phases of civil emergency planning.

The Agency represented the United States at the 11th and 12th meetings of the Civil Defense Committee, which was created in 1952 to promote the development of national civil defense programs and the exchange of information among member nations.

2. *Cooperation With Canada.*—Coordination of civil defense operations between Canada and the United States was facilitated by an agreement entered into by the two countries in 1951, and the establishment of the Joint United States–Canada Civil Defense Committee. At its sixth meeting held in Ottawa in May, the Joint Committee agreed to set up an arrangement for day-to-day liaison between technical representatives of the two countries for such programs as training and education, communications, warning, survival planning, welfare, health, engineering and shelter design, research and development, emergency legislation, industrial survival, radiological defense, continuity of government, resources and requirements, and public information.

3. *Exchange Program.*—In July 1957, 30 civil defense officials from 10 European countries took part in the Agency's foreign observer program at the AEC Nevada Test Site. In addition, shelters designed and financed by the French and West German governments were tested. Following the test series, technicians from those governments visited the Nevada Test Site in December for a postshot inspection of the shelters.

In addition to the foreign officials who attended the test series in Nevada, the Agency arranged for staff briefings and consultation for 10 civil defense officials visiting the United States from Australia, Denmark, Germany, Great Britain, and Sweden. Seven Canadians and one Australian attended Agency training courses during the year. As part of the program to exchange civil defense equipment for testing and evaluation purposes, the Agency loaned radiological instruments to the Portuguese Government, and protective masks to the Governments of Switzerland, Norway, and Sweden.

Approximately 330 requests for technical and public information literature, and the loan of films, were received from national or diplomatic representatives of other Governments, including Austria, Australia, Burma, India, Iran, Israel, Ireland, Lebanon, Luxembourg, Malta, Mexico, Pakistan, Spain, Sweden, Switzerland, and the NATO nations.

AMERICAN NATIONAL RED CROSS

As part of its program of training groups and individuals to be prepared to meet emergencies, the Red Cross trained 975,000 persons in first aid, 240,000 persons in home care of the sick and injured, and thousands in emergency mass feeding techniques.[1]

The Red Cross also worked with FCDA and other Federal agencies on the development of a nationwide blood-procurement system.

The ANRC maintained a full-time liaison representative at FCDA National Headquarters and at two of the Agency's regional headquarters, and part-time liaison service at the other FCDA regional offices.

CIVIL DEFENSE ADVISORY COUNCIL

The Civil Defense Advisory Council met three times during the year. Two of the meetings (September 1957 and January 1958) were devoted to detailed reviews of drafts of the National Civil Defense Plan.[2] At the third meeting (June 1958) the Council considered the merger of FCDA and ODM, civil defense appropriation requests for

---

[1] National statistics on the exact number of graduates of the "Basic Course in Emergency Mass Feeding" which was developed jointly by FCDA and ANRC, were not available at the end of the fiscal year.

[2] See ch. 1, Planning.

fiscal year 1950, the National Policy on Shelters, and the status of the National Civil Defense Plan.

The President appointed 3 new members to the Council, replacing members whose terms had expired, and reappointed 3 members. At the close of the year the following were Council members:

Hon. Leo A. Hoegh, Chairman.

Hon. J. Caleb Boggs, Governor of Delaware (reappointed).

Hon. Luther H. Hodges, Governor of North Carolina (new member).

Mrs. Hiram Cole Houghton, Red Oak, Iowa (new member).

Hon. John B. Hynes, Mayor of Boston (reappointed).

Hon. Goodwin J. Knight, Governor of California (reappointed).

Maj. Gen. Otto L. Nelson, Jr., Vice President, New York Life Insurance Co.

Hon. Okey L. Patteson, former Governor of West Virginia.

Hon. P. Kenneth Peterson, Mayor of Minneapolis (new member).

Mr. George J. Richardson, Special Assistant to the President, AFL–CIO.

Hon. Clifford E. Rishell, Mayor of Oakland.

Mr. Robert E. Smith, Houston, Tex.

Mrs. Charles W. Weis, Jr., Rochester, N.Y.

CIVIL DEFENSE COORDINATING BOARD

The Civil Defense Coordinating Board, composed of the representatives of 17 Federal agencies,[3] met 7 times during the year. Five of the seven meetings were devoted entirely to a careful study and discussion of the National Civil Defense Plan.[4] Other important agenda items included discussions on the coordination of passive research activities in the Federal Government, and the emergency functions of the Federal Government.

NATIONAL ADVISORY COUNCIL ON RURAL CIVIL DEFENSE

The National Advisory Council on Rural Civil Defense, established in 1955 to assist in the development of civil defense programs in the nonurban areas of the Nation, met twice during the year for discussions on radiological defense, mass feeding problems, stockpiling legislation, the National Civil Defense Plan,[5] the Agency's continuity of State

---

[3] The Board was established on May 11, 1955, by Executive Order 10611.

[4] See ch. 1, Planning.

[5] See ch. 1, Planning.

and local government program,[6] and a proposed civil defense public information program for nonurban areas.

RELIGIOUS GROUPS

Information and guidance on the Agency's plans and programs were made available to churches and clergymen through personal conferences, group meetings, and printed material. More than 2,000 religious leaders attended 19 major civil defense meetings during the year.

The National Religious Advisory Committee, which is composed of church executives representing all of the major denominations, met twice to discuss various aspects of the role of the clergy in civil defense. Seventy-five national church executives, representing 40 denominations, met in Washington in May and adopted resolutions in support of civil defense. Other meetings with religious groups were held in Georgia, Michigan, Minnesota, Oregon, Tennessee, and Rhode Island.

The Agency assisted Canada in the development of its first staff college course in civil defense for clergymen.

WOMEN'S ORGANIZATIONS

The National Women's Advisory Committee, composed of the presidents of 75 national women's organizations and 26 members-at-large, held its annual meeting in October. The Committee approved the new National Policy on Shelters[7] and was active in urging the passage of the Durham Bill.[8] In addition, such organizations as the American Legion Auxiliary, Dorcas Societies of the Seventh-day Adventist Church, Federation of Women's Clubs, Home Demonstration Clubs, and the Auxiliary to the Veterans of Foreign Wars, and many others made extensive use of the Agency's *Home Preparedness Workshop Kit* for group leaders, and organized courses in first aid and home nursing.

BUSINESS AND INDUSTRIAL GROUPS

A number of business and industrial groups included civil defense planning in their yearly activities. For example, the Los Angeles Chamber of Commerce sponsored a Western Industrial Survival Conference at which prominent industrial representatives from seven

---

[6] See ch. 2, Continuity of Government.
[7] See ch. 3, Radiological Defense.
[8] See ch. 1, Planning.

Losing My Religion

The report at left mentions two thousand religious leaders attending civil defense meetings in 1958. Many among them were ready to play devil's advocate against those who would put a positive spin on nuclear weapons. However, it was risky at the time to openly defy the U.S. government's optimistic messages about the survivability of nuclear war.

The media often helped spur the backlash against any nuclear naysayers. In 1957, for instance, *Time* magazine condemned the newly formed National Committee for a Sane Nuclear Policy for lending credence to "the horror stories of nuclear fallout [being spread by] the sworn enemies of religion, liberty and peace," or in the words of the House Committee on Un-American Activities, "the black hand of the Communist conspiracy."

If this were true, then one of "the sworn enemies of religion" was religion itself—or, more specifically, the Catholic publication *The Commonweal*, which printed this bit of anti-nuke blasphemy in 1961: "Not even the most optimistic civil defense advocates hold out any possibility that those in target areas could be saved. Those cowering in the subway or munching fall-out biscuits in basements would be killed by radiation or blast, or else die of the carbon monoxide fumes from the fires that raged outside."

It was not the first time the Catholic Church had stirred things up regarding this politically charged issue. In 1956, when then–presidential candidate Adlai Stevenson endorsed anti-bomb statements put forward by the *Catholic Worker* newspaper and the Federation of Atomic Scientists, Vice President Richard Nixon called it "catastrophic nonsense."

When Stevenson died in 1965, the *Bulletin of Atomic Scientists* eulogized him: "(M)any argued that in our world of violence and strife, no man of his wisdom, conscience, and self-doubt . . . could be elected president." The bulletin recalled him as a man who was "willing to subordinate national interests . . . to the overriding need for common salvation."

CUT OUT
AND CARRY
THESE SMALL CARDS

REMEMBER THESE **CD** WARNING SIGNALS

RED ALERT

EXPECT AN ATTACK ANY MOMENT

SIRENS, HORNS OR WHISTLES

ONE 3-MINUTE WARBLING SIGNAL
OR SERIES OF SHORT BLASTS

FOLLOW OFFICIAL INSTRUCTIONS ONLY

ALL-CLEAR SIGNAL
ENEMY AIRCRAFT NO LONGER IN THE AREA

| 1 MINUTE BLAST | 2 MINUTES SILENCE | 1 MINUTE BLAST | 2 MINUTES SILENCE | 1 MINUTE BLAST |

THREE 1-MINUTE BLASTS
TWO MINUTES OF SILENCE BETWEEN

PUBLISHED BY THE FEDERAL CIVIL DEFENSE ADMINISTRATION

Civil Defense Air Raid card 1950s. *Utah State Historical Society*

western States discussed industrial survival planning. In addition, civil defense topics were discussed at the annual meetings of such organizations as the Aircraft Industry Association, the American Society for Industrial Security, State manufacturers' associations, State and regional safety organizations affiliated with the National Safety Council, and Chambers of Commerce.

AFL–CIO LABOR ADVISORY COMMITTEE

The AFL–CIO Labor Advisory Committee met three times during the year to review and make recommendations on the National Civil Defense Plan and the Agency's Skilled Manpower Cataloging Project at Grand Rapids, Mich.

The Grand Rapids project, aimed at finding skills in the local labor force that would be needed in immediate postdisaster operations, was completed. Among the findings were the following: (a) about 7 percent of the normal working force has emergency assignments (e.g., police, fire, and other governmental employees); (b) about 4.5 percent of the normal work force is composed of members of the building and construction trades who could be assigned to postdisaster jobs similar to the work they normally do; (c) about 7.4 percent of the working force in manufacturing, public utility, and similar services has skills that would be needed in immediate postdisaster periods.

The committee recommended that similar skills cataloging projects be carried out in at least two other cities.

What's in a Name?

Operation Survival wasn't just the title of a 1958 educational comic book for kids; in March 1960, the same name would be used for a set of U.S. Army Medical Department nuclear emergency doctrines. According to the U.S. Army's Office of Medical History, the purpose of these doctrines

> was to underline the necessity of emergency medical care training for Army troops to ensure their survival on the nuclear battlefield. In demonstrating the techniques of emergency medical care and their relationship to various levels of division organization, three main problems were highlighted: (1) In the field, as in garrison, the initial care to casualties will frequently be self-aid or buddy-care, (2) the logistics burden imposed by mass casualty situations represents a serious drain on a division's manpower and equipment, and (3) a disparity exists between medical means and medical requirements within the infantry battle group. Subsequent maneuvers throughout the decade continued to demonstrate the problems of medical support to nonmedical military commanders.

The U.S. Army Medical Department stopped using the operational name after its reorganization in the late 1960s, but that wasn't the end of this catchy title. In 1970, the Liberty Lobby, with ties to the Nixon Administration, launched an "Operation Survival" fundraiser, with its stated goal being to raise $400,000 annually "to help prevent the U.S. climate from deteriorating into further chaos," according to the lobby's policy chairman at the time, Robert Bartell.

The Anti-Defamation League of B'nai B'rith, however, reported that the Liberty Lobby's more circumspect goal was "to finance a military dictatorship in the U.S.," as reported in *Mother Jones* magazine in April 1981. Operation Survival might have met its financial goals, but that military dictatorship has yet to take shape as of this printing.

As for the Operation Survival educational comic book, copies of it are currently up for auction on eBay.

THANK GOODNESS, YOU CHILDREN ARE BACK!

SWITCH ON THE RADIO, JIM!

ATTENTION, PLEASE! THIS IS A NATIONAL EMERGENCY! THE AIR FORCE HAS ANNOUNCED THAT ENEMY AIRCRAFT ARE APPROACHING THIS COMMUNITY. AN ATTACK IS IMMINENT. GO TO THE NEAREST AVAILABLE SHELTER AND STAY THERE! THIS IS NOT A TEST! THIS COMMUNITY MAY BE UNDER ENEMY AIR ATTACK WITHIN MINUTES. GO QUICKLY BUT CALMLY TO THE NEAREST SHELTER. TAKE A PORTABLE RADIO AND EMERGENCY FOOD WITH YOU, IF POSSIBLE. OBEY YOUR AUTHORITIES. FURTHER INSTRUCTIONS WILL COME TO YOU AT 640 OR 1240 ON YOUR RADIO DIAL. THIS STATION IS NOW LEAVING THE AIR. KEEP YOUR RADIO TUNED TO 640 OR 1240.

TIME PASSES...

WE'VE BEEN HERE FOR HOURS AND I HAVEN'T HEARD ANY BOMB EXPLOSIONS! LET'S GO OUT AND SEE WHAT'S HAPPENED IF ANYTHING!

WE STAY RIGHT HERE UNTIL WE GET AN ALL CLEAR. BOMBS COULD HAVE FALLEN ON A TARGET AREA MANY MILES OFF--WE STILL MIGHT BE IN DANGER FROM RADIOACTIVE FALLOUT!

JUST WHAT IS THIS FALLOUT, ANYWAY, DAD?

FALLOUT IS WHAT WE CALL THE RADIOACTIVE PARTICLES IN THE MUSHROOM CLOUD WHEN AN H-BOMB EXPLODES NEAR THE EARTH.

WHEN AN *ATOMIC* OR *HYDROGEN* BOMB IS EXPLODED CLOSE TO THE GROUND, THOUSANDS OF TONS OF EARTH AND ROCK ARE TURNED INTO PIECES AS SMALL AS DUST. THESE SMALL PIECES ARE SUCKED UPWARD IN A GREAT MUSHROOM CLOUD SOMETIMES TO A HEIGHT OF *80,000 FEET OR MORE.*

A-BOMB   H-BOMB   THUNDERSTO

THE PARTICLES ARE THEN MADE RADIOACTIVE AND FALL BACK TO EARTH OVER A *WIDE AREA.* THEY CAN BE CARRIED *GREAT DISTANCES.* FOR INSTANCE, IF YOU ARE AS MUCH AS 200 MILES DOWNWIND FROM THE SCENE OF SUCH AN EXPLOSION YOU CAN BE EXPOSED TO THE DANGERS OF RADIO-ACTIVE FALLOUT THAT'S ROUGHLY THE DISTANCE BETWEEN *WASHINGTON* AND *NEW YORK.*

WASHINGTON   NEW YORK

SURVEY INSTRUMENTS

THE *ONLY WAY* TO FIND OUT IF AN AREA HAS BEEN MADE DANGEROUS FROM RADIOACTIVE FALLOUT IS TO USE *SPECIAL INSTRUMENTS* THAT WILL REACT TO RADIOACTIVITY... HERE ARE SOME PICTURES OF THEM.

SURVEY ME[TERS]

GEIGER COUNTER

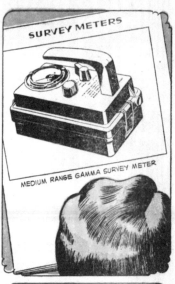

SURVEY METERS

MEDIUM RANGE GAMMA SURVEY METER

HIGH RANGE BETA-GAMMA SURVEY METER

THESE SURVEY INSTRUMENTS MEASURE THE DEGREE OF *RADIOACTIVITY* PRESENT IN AN AREA. JUST AS THE NEEDLE ON A SPEEDOMETER SHOWS HOW FAST A CAR IS TRAVELING, THE INDICATOR ON THESE INSTRUMENTS TELLS *HOW MUCH* RADIOACTIVITY THERE IS.

NOW, IF YOU HAPPENED TO BE IN AN AREA THAT HAD BEEN MADE RADIOACTIVE BY FALL-OUT, YOU WOULD NEED TO KNOW HOW MUCH RADIOACTIVITY *YOU YOURSELF* HAD ABSORBED. THERE IS ANOTHER INSTRUMENT THAT MEASURES THIS. IT'S CALLED A *DOSIMETER.*

SURVEY METERS

DOSIMETER

THE DOSIMETER COULD BE COMPARED TO THE MILEAGE COUNTER ON A CAR WHICH TELLS *HOW FAR* THE CAR HAS GONE. THE DOSIMETER TELLS *HOW MUCH* RADIOACTIVITY YOU HAVE TAKEN IN OR ABSORBED.

WOW, THEY SURE GOT THINGS FIGURED OUT. HOW SOON CAN WE LEAVE THE SHELTER, DAD?

NOT UNTIL WE GET WORD THAT IT'S *SAFE*. RADIOLOGICAL MONITOR-ING TEAMS USING THE INSTRUMENTS SHOWED YOU WILL FIRST *MAKE SURE* WHETHER OR NOT THERE IS EVIDENCE OF FALLOUT PRESENT. WE MAY HAVE A *LONG WAIT*.

TRY YOUR HAND AT THIS PUZZLE AND SEE HOW MUCH YOU KNOW.

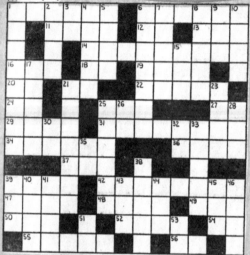

ACROSS

1 Place of refuge during a tornado
6 What an alarm indicates
11 Eastern continent
12 Elevated train
13 Rural Electrification Administration (abbr.)
14 What this puzzle is if you can't solve it
16 Before
18 A printer's measure
19 Not odd
20 Musical note
21 Advertisement
22 Where birds go for shelter
24 Road (abbr.)
25 Used in chemical warfare
27 He should know about Civil Defense
29 Objectives
31 The _____ Red Cross
34 He can help in emergencies
36 The size of the atom
37 Terminate
39 Term used in radio communications
42 Volcanic disaster
47 Your city is prepared to fight this
48 To nominate
49 Untruth
50 May be needed in airing a bomb shelter
52 An instrument of alarm
54 French definite article
55 Matter of law
56 Word of approval

DOWN

1 "640-1240" Emergency broadcasting system
2 The kind of person first-aid may help
3 Left side (abbr.)
4 Helped
5 Source of water supply
6 Civil
7 Alert Today— _____ tomorrow
8 Deep, guttural sound
9 Elongated fish
10 Fixed ratio
15 "These" in French
17 Communication vital to Civil Defense
21 Strict in living
23 A flood can wash out this part of a bridge
25 A well-cultivated tract of land
26 Morning hour
28 One no matter which
30 Program director
32 Neuter pronoun
33 _____ Defense
35 A good defense slogan is "Carry _____"
38 Unauthenticated report
39 Away
40 Small bottle
41 Sea eagle
43 Tattered cloth
44 Writing implement
45 Lubricate
46 Require
51 She should know about Civil Defense
53 A green traffic sign

ANSWER ON PAGE 31

QUIZ

1. (Circle the correct answer.) In order to cope with any type of disaster, a community must (have many people) (be prepared) (wait for the armed forces).

2. List at least 6 agencies of your local government that must be ready to protect the people of a community in time of disaster.

   1. _____
   2. _____
   3. _____
   4. _____
   5. _____
   6. _____

3. Name at least 5 basic items that families should have in order to be prepared for any type of disaster.

   1. _____
   2. _____
   3. _____
   4. _____
   5. _____

4. What is radioactive fallout?_____
   _____

5. Name 2 instruments that are used for measuring radioactivity.

   1. _____
   2. _____

6. What is a dosimeter?_____
   _____

7. List 4 new ideas that you have learned from reading this booklet.

   1. _____
   2. _____
   3. _____
   4. _____

Warning sign on a fence surrounding the Trinity Site in New Mexico where the first nuclear bomb was exploded.

II.
The Rise of the Nukes
1960s

In order to better understand the physics of nuclear weapons and develop new technological innovations, tests were conducted. Originally these tests were atmospheric: above ground, in the air, underwater, or on the surface of the water. American testing moved from New Mexico to islands in the South Pacific before finally moving to the Nevada Test Site north of Las Vegas.

Both adversaries developed delivery systems for the nuclear weapons. The Americans developed the Strategic Air Command, ready and able to destroy the Soviet Union with a fleet of aircraft that reached a maximum number of over 1,500 bombers and over 700 refueling tankers in the early 1960s. An Aerospace Defense Command defended the United States with fighters and antiaircraft missiles. The Soviets built fewer bombers, but their Air Defense Forces was larger than the American version. In the 1950s, ballistic missile technology rapidly developed. Building on the efforts by the Germans to produce V-2 rockets during World War II, the MRBM (medium-range ballistic missile), with a range of 200 miles, was developed. The IRBM (intermediate-range ballistic missile) quickly followed, with a range of up to 1,500 miles. The ICBM (intercontinental ballistic missile) was operational by the end of the decade, having a range of over 6,000 miles, meaning that missiles launched from either the Soviet Union or the United States could reach enemy territory.

The United States initially built many more bombers and ICBMs than the Soviets. The Americans also had allies closer to the western part of the Soviet Union, where shorter-range missiles (IRBMs) were placed in Turkey and Britain. The Soviets were completely outmatched in the late 1950s. Cuba then fell to a revolution that turned communist, and Fidel Castro asked for Soviet protection. In 1962 the Soviets sneaked in troops, tactical nuclear weapons, and strategic nuclear weapons in the form of MRBM and IRBM missiles. An American U-2 spy plane found the missile sites only weeks before they became active. The Americans concluded that they could not allow these missiles to remain there, and the Cuban Missile Crisis began. Over thirteen days in October the world grew ever more tense as the Americans imposed a quarantine to block any more Soviet missiles from arriving in Cuba, and America also prepared to invade the island. Americans scrambled to build personal fallout shelters, a desperate solution that might ensure survival of individual families for a time.

Finally the Soviets blinked and agreed to withdraw if the Americans promised not to invade Cuba and would remove their missiles from Turkey. This was easy enough for the Americans to agree to, since Kennedy did not want to invade Cuba and the Americans already planned to withdraw the Jupiter IRBMs from Turkey because they were obsolete. The new Minuteman ICBM had made strategic missiles in allied countries unnecessary. This crisis was the closest the world has ever come to a general nuclear war.

In their eagerness to see what this new toy could do, scientists created numerous different designs that led to nuclear weapons being delivered by artillery shells, small tactical missiles, large strategic missiles, depth charges, torpedoes, ground-launched antiaircraft missiles, air-to-air missiles, or even bombs delivered via a large backpack. One of the reasons for the large number of nuclear devices in the American and Soviet stockpiles was to provide weapons for all these different delivery systems. Many of these weapons had smaller yields, and the category of tactical nuclear weapons was born, as opposed to the larger strategic weapons that were designed to end civilizations if used in great enough quantity. Military and political theorists argued that the use of tactical nuclear weapons did not mean that an imaginary threshold had been crossed that would automatically lead to full-scale strategic nuclear warfare.

While both superpowers rapidly increased their stockpiles of nuclear weapons and built new delivery systems, the question of how to fight a nuclear war became ever more pressing. Were nuclear weapons just big bombs, or did they constitute an entirely new form of warfare? Because the Soviets maintained armies much larger than the Americans and their allies in Western Europe, the Americans relied on nuclear weapons to ensure that a conventional war in Europe would remain unthinkable. They promised "massive retaliation" in the event of a Soviet invasion of Western Europe. As the Soviet nuclear stockpile increased in size, the term *MAD* (mutual assured destruction) came to describe the military doctrine that both sides followed. If one superpower tried to destroy the other, enough nuclear weapons would survive to ensure the complete destruction of the attacker's home nation. MAD drove the efforts to build even more nuclear weapons and find ways to hide or protect them, such as armed bombers waiting on alert or already airborne, flying in rotation; missiles snug in hardened silos that were difficult to destroy; or submarines that prowled the world's oceans waiting to retaliate for a homeland already turned into a radioactive wasteland.

The following section includes more literature designed to give civilians on the homefront peace of mind, which would be harder to come by after the anxious thirteen days of the Cuban Missile Crisis. Corporate America even pitched in, as with Detroit Edison's distribution of Home Preparedness Files to all its employees in 1962. These envelopes consisted of civil defense brochures, checklists, and information cards on what to do to protect your family when the warning sirens start to blare.

Do-it-yourselfers will appreciate *Fallout Protection for Homes with Basements* (1966), a guide for the home handyman for building a personal shelter for the family where a public one isn't easily accessed. It includes an inspiring message from President Lyndon B. Johnson that emphasizes the "clear value" of saving civilian lives in the event of World War III, and tips such as adding pillows and wood frames around concrete-block benches for a convenient and comfortable "finishing touch."

This section concludes with *In Time of Emergency: A Citizen's Handbook on Nuclear Attack* (1968), which updates and expands on information from earlier handouts, especially in the category of shelter supplies, first aid, sanitation, and "personal convenience items" such as cosmetics, playing cards, and books and magazines "if space permits."

CIVIL
PREPARED...

PREPARE...
Your family...
C...

contents:

family
preparedness

warning
signals

CIVIL DEFENSE
INFORMATION
FOR EMP...

CIVIL DEFENSE
HOME PREPAREDNESS FILE

DISCUSS CONTENTS WITH YOUR FAMILY
ADD YOUR CHECK LIST AND ASSIGNMENTS
KEEP FILE HANDY - REVIEW PERIODICALLY
TACK UP REMINDER CARD IN CONVENIENT PLACE

Prepared for Employes by
The Detroit Edison Company
Civil Defense Department

The Ultimate Employee Benefits Package

In a March 2007 article, Greg Gordon of McClatchy Newspapers reported that "absent a major preparedness push, the U.S. response to a mushroom cloud could be worse than the debacle after Hurricane Katrina, possibly contributing to civil disorder and costing thousands of lives."

According to the article, "The government has yet to launch an educational program, akin to the Cold War–era civil defense campaign promoting fallout shelters, to teach Americans how to shield themselves from radiation."

Today's government, in short, is following the "ignorance is bliss" doctrine when it comes to nuclear survival. However, if it does decide to revisit the efforts of the past, it could do worse than entrusting companies like Detroit Edison to pitch in, as the company did in 1962 with the following "Home Preparedness File," distributed to all of the company's employees in December of that year—a nice addition to their Christmas bonuses.

Shallow underground burst. *United States Atomic Energy Commission*

CIVIL DEFENSE
INFORMATION
FOR EMPLOYES
AND FAMILIES

THE DETROIT EDISON COMPANY
CIVIL DEFENSE DEPARTMENT
December 1962

FOREWORD

Just as your department in the Company has formulated a Civil Defense plan for the protection of all their employes while at work, so should you plan for the protection of yourself and your family at home. To assist you in setting up your own preparedness program, the attached booklets will provide the basic information you need. The suggestions in this pamphlet will also help answer some of your questions about your home program. If you require additional information on shelters or other emergency procedures your local Civil Defense agency will provide the material.

SUGGESTED STEPS FOR FAMILY PREPAREDNESS IN CIVIL DEFENSE EMERGENCY

General Discussion with Your Family

Read Civil Defense booklets enclosed. These have been selected from many available from the Office of Civil Defense to give you general information for discussion on what Civil Defense means, why it is necessary, and how you can prepare for living under emergency conditions.

Explain to your family the Company instructions that apply to you while you are at work. Also make it clear to them that you will be in a Company shelter or other shelter area until it is safe to travel. Outline their responsibilities when you are not at home.

Find out where your local alert siren is located and describe the Civil Defense signals so all members of the family will know what they are. Stress to them the importance of being more conscious of the various siren signals so that when an alert comes they will pay attention.

Evacuation procedures are not recommended by Civil Defense Authorities in our area -- the shelter program is being emphasized as offering the best protection.

Community shelters are also being set up in most city areas -- check your own Civil Defense program to see if a community shelter is available for your family. If a public shelter is preferable for your use, clearly establish the best route from your house.

Discuss your local school plan for handling students during school hours. Some schools will send them home or ask parents to pick them up. This will require careful advance planning on your part to see that it works smoothly and everyone in your family understands the system.

Read carefully the instructions on seeking shelter or taking protective measures if an alert sounds while you or members of your family are away from home. Be sure all family members know what to do for their immediate protection. The worry and uncertainty of the whereabouts of absent members can be offset by the assurance that they are really better off seeking the best available shelter. As soon as conditions warrant, they can rejoin the family.

SPECIFIC STEPS

Decide on the best shelter area for your family. If in your home, determine how far you want to go in shelter and storage preparation. Make your own check list of things to do and assignments for your family. Keep it handy. It might be well to set up periodic training exercises for family participation.

Certain minimum steps can be taken by everyone and the following are suggestions for some basic preparations:

1. Have some cooking and eating utensils stored in your shelter area. Your camping or picnic set will usually serve the purpose.

2. Water from your hot water heater will supplement your water supply -- check to be sure you can use the lower drain. If your outside water supply is cut off, also turn off the heating unit on your water heater. Water supply from underground wells need not be cut off. It is also advisable to fill your bathtub before going to the shelter area.

3. Instruct your family to take all available food including canned goods to the shelter area. Freezers and refrigerators in the basement will keep food safe and provide added storage.

4. Take blankets, pillows, extra clothing and at least one mattress -- if you have air mattresses, sleeping bags, or camp cots, store them in or near the shelter area. Folding chairs and tables are also convenient for shelter use.

5. Take a radio, flashlight, first aid kit, and any medical supplies required.

6. Consider what you will take for care of your children, including material to keep them occupied.

7. Close doors, pull shades and turn off all unnecessary equipment.

8. It is not necessary to disconnect your electric service.

OTHER REMINDERS

Emphasize to your family that knowing what to do and taking time to do it will help eliminate panic and make their stay in the shelter area more comfortable.

Telephone lines are needed for Civil Defense purposes, so advise your family not to make or expect phone calls.

Advise everyone to stay in the shelter until notified by radio that it is safe to leave. If your house is entirely closed, limited movement may be permitted within the house if essential to get additional equipment. It is advisable however, to wait as long as possible and make your trip short.

During the recovery period advise your family to stay in the house as much as possible and try to stay self-sufficient as a family. Civil Defense agencies and business organizations will be busy restoring essential services and travel will be limited. If you are at home prepare to report back to work as instructed by your department or wait for a phone or radio call for instructions. If you have been in a shelter away from home, you may return home, if possible, before reporting.

SHELTER SUPPLIES

Not every item on this chart is vital to life. (The most essential ones are outlined in color.) But even though you might be able to leave your shelter briefly after a day or two, you should prepare to be *completely* self-sustaining for at least two weeks.

EATING UTENSILS AND FOOD

EATING UTENSILS — CUPS — NAPKINS — BOTTLE OPENER — CAN OPENER — POCKET KNIFE — MEASURING CUP — PAPER PLATES — PAN — WATER — FOOD AND CONTAINERS

CLOTHING AND BEDDING

SEWING KIT — SLEEPING BAGS — BLANKETS — EXTRA CLOTHING

SANITATION AND MEDICAL SUPPLIES

DISINFECTANT — GARBAGE CAN — PAPER TOWELS — FIRST AID KIT — SANITARY NAPKINS — EMERGENCY TOILET — TOILET PAPER — HUMAN WASTE — NEWSPAPERS — SOAP — PLASTIC AND PAPER BAGS

The one essential is water; most people can live no more than four days without it. The minimum for a shelter is one quart of fluid per person per day; if space is available near the shelter, a gallon of water a day per person would provide for your comfort, including washing.

Some items, such as tools, should be kept handy but need not be inside the shelter itself.

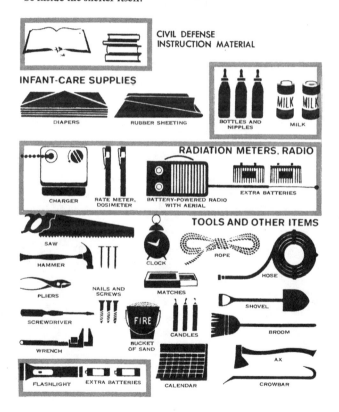

CIVIL DEFENSE
INSTRUCTION MATERIAL

INFANT-CARE SUPPLIES

DIAPERS

RUBBER SHEETING

BOTTLES AND NIPPLES

MILK

RADIATION METERS, RADIO

CHARGER

RATE METER, DOSIMETER

BATTERY-POWERED RADIO WITH AERIAL

EXTRA BATTERIES

TOOLS AND OTHER ITEMS

SAW

HAMMER

CLOCK

ROPE

HOSE

PLIERS

NAILS AND SCREWS

MATCHES

SHOVEL

SCREWDRIVER

BUCKET OF SAND

CANDLES

BROOM

WRENCH

FIRE

FLASHLIGHT

EXTRA BATTERIES

CALENDAR

AX

CROWBAR

28

2 WARNING SIGNALS

There are two distinct public action signals.

1. a steady blast of 3 to 5 minutes means: Attack Probable

take action as directed by your local government

Tune your AM radio to a CONELRAD frequency (640 or 1240) for official directions. Proceed according to your community's emergency action plan. Don't use the telephone.

2. warbling tone or short blasts for 3 minutes means: Attack Imminent

take cover immediately in best available shelter

in a building— if there is no prepared shelter, go to basement or to an interior room on first floor. Stay until you are told to leave.

outdoors or in a car – go to the nearest shelter. If you cannot reach prepared shelter, lie face down on the ground or crouch on the floor of the car.

16

CONELRAD INSTRUCTIONS 3

Following an "attack alert," all radio and television stations will be silenced to deny navigational assistance to enemy aircraft in reaching targets.

Certain radio stations will return to the air on low power, broadcasting official information and instructions on two wavelengths only—640 and 1240.

640

1240

The changeover to CONELRAD takes a few minutes. Do not be alarmed by the radio silence in the meanwhile. Stay tuned to one of these numbers—640 or 1240—and follow the announced instructions carefully.

17

CIVIL DEFENSE
PREPAREDNESS AT HOME

PREPARE:

Your family plan --- your shelter area.
Check list for supplies.
Assign responsibilities to family members
for the following:

    Food - bedding - clothing - medical
       and children's supplies - radio -
       flashlight.
    Close house - pull shades - fill bathtub.

ACTION:

When WARNING SIGNALS sound---Pay
Attention but Don't Panic!

A STEADY BLAST OF 3 TO 5 MINUTES
Means: ATTACK PROBABLE---Put your
family plan in action. Tune your radio
to CONELRAD - 640 or 1240 - for official
information and directions. Don't use
telephone.

WAILING TONE OR SHORT BLASTS FOR
3 MINUTES
Means: ATTACK IMMINENT---Finish
last minute preparations and proceed to
shelter. Stay there until you get the word
to leave.

NUCLEAR BOMB EFFECTS COMPUTER

(Revised Edition, 1962)

based on data from

"The Effects of Nuclear Weapons"

developed by

The Lovelace Foundation

under contract to

The Division of Biology and Medicine

of the

U.S. Atomic Energy Commission

This computer is sold separately by the Superintendent of Documents for $1.00 and is not included in the price of the book, "The Effects of Nuclear Weapons" which sells for $3.00.

A "Nuclear Bomb Effects Computer" was affixed inside the back cover of *The Effects of Nuclear Weapons*, a report prepared by the U.S. Department of Defense and published by the U.S. Atomic Energy Commission in April 1962. *United States Government Printing Office*

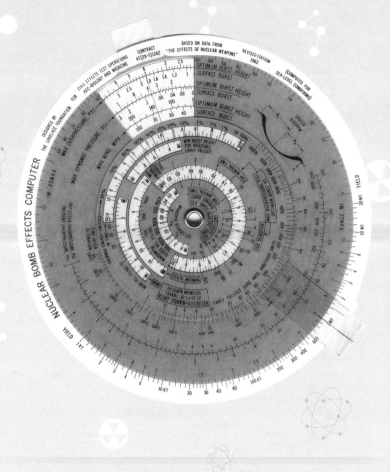

On these two pages: The Nuclear Bomb Effects Computer (front and back). Among other things, it could be used to determine the velocity of window glass—which can be deadly as flying shrapnel—in feet per second, and the fallout dose rate at various explosive yields and distances over a period of thirty days. It also charts the survivability of

radiation at various exposures. For instance, at over 5,000 rems (rems are the standard unit to measure radiation dosage), which is the immediate dose of a one-megaton yield at a distance of about 1.25 miles, it calculates a 100 percent personnel fatality rate from radiation poisoning after seven days. *United States Government Printing Office*

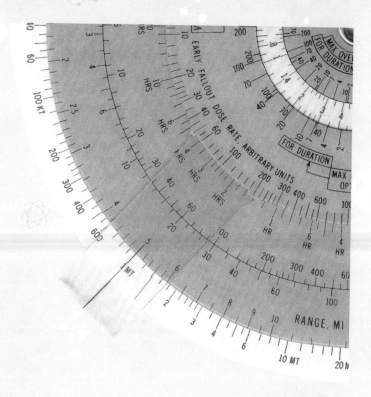

Measuring the effects of a one-megaton blast at a range of five miles. The point at which the curved lines cross, based on yield and distance, determines the initial thermal radiation (essentially, the heat transfer from the nuclear blast to surrounding objects) and nuclear radiation.

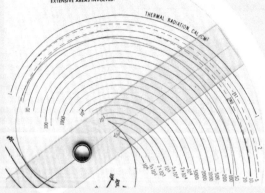

DASHED LINES INDICATE:
1ST DEGREE BURNS—SIMILAR TO
SUNBURN WITH NO BLISTERING
2ND DEGREE BURNS—BLISTERING;
SERIOUS IF FACE OR
EXTENSIVE AREAS INVOLVED.

THERMAL RADIATION, CAL/CM²

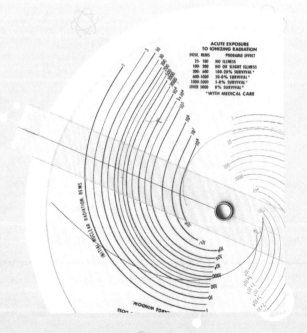

ACUTE EXPOSURE
TO IONIZING RADIATION

DOSE, REMS	PROBABLE EFFECT
25- 100	NO ILLNESS
100- 200	NO OR SLIGHT ILLNESS
200- 600	100-20% SURVIVAL*
600-1000	20-0% SURVIVAL*
1000-5000	5-0% SURVIVAL*
OVER 5000	0% SURVIVAL*

*WITH MEDICAL CARE

INITIAL NUCLEAR RADIATION, REMS

LARGE WINDOW.

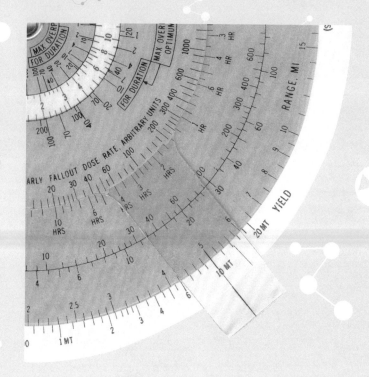

Measuring the effects of a ten-megaton blast at a range of five miles—the cold calculus of destruction rendered in the precise numbers and lines of a slide rule . . . and it spins!

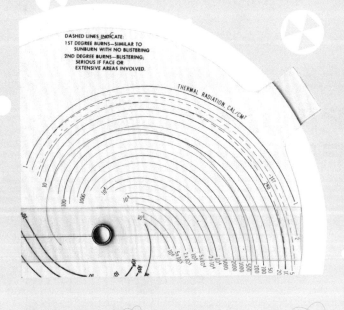

DASHED LINES INDICATE:
1ST DEGREE BURNS—SIMILAR TO
SUNBURN WITH NO BLISTERING
2ND DEGREE BURNS—BLISTERING;
SERIOUS IF FACE OR
EXTENSIVE AREAS INVOLVED.

THERMAL RADIATION, CAL/CM?

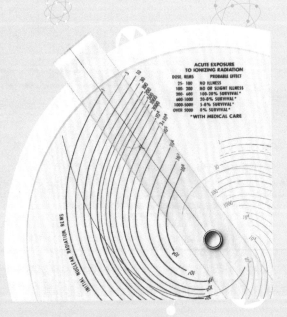

ACUTE EXPOSURE
TO IONIZING RADIATION

DOSE, REMS	PROBABLE EFFECT
25- 100	NO ILLNESS
100- 200	NO OR SLIGHT ILLNESS
200- 600	100-20% SURVIVAL*
600-1000	20-5% SURVIVAL*
1000-5000	5-0% SURVIVAL*
OVER 5000	0% SURVIVAL*

*WITH MEDICAL CARE

INITIAL NUCLEAR RADIATION, REMS

FALLOUT PROTECTION FOR...

HOMES

WITH BASEMENTS

See back cover for your individual Home Protection Factor

  DEPARTMENT OF DEFENSE • OFFICE OF CIVIL DEFENSE
JULY 1966 H-12

U.S. DEPARTMENT OF COMMERCE
BUREAU OF THE CENSUS
WASHINGTON, D.C. 20233

OFFICE OF THE DIRECTOR

Dear Fellow Citizen:

Thank you for participating in the recent Home Fallout Protection Survey.

On the back cover of the enclosed booklet are the results of the analysis of your home, based on the information you reported on the Home Survey Questionnaire. Details concerning the analysis are explained in the booklet which also includes, for your consideration, suggested methods for increasing the amount of protection available if this is desired.

According to the Department of Defense, Office of Civil Defense, in the event of nuclear attack you may have to rely heavily on the protection your home provides against radioactive fallout. If public shelter is available to you in your community, the degree of protection afforded by your home will assist you in deciding whether you would prefer to remain at home or use public shelter. Your State or local government is, or will be, engaged in planning the use of all public shelters. When these Community Shelter Plans are completed, your local government will be in a position to inform you of the most effective use of shelter resources in your community.

Your cooperation in this survey is deeply appreciated.

Sincerely yours,

A. Ross Eckler

A. Ross Eckler
Director
Bureau of the Census

Enclosure

NOTE: *Please include your complete identification number as shown on the top line of the address label on all correspondence.*

FORM DS-200 (6-28-66)
USCOMM-DC

☆ U.S. GOVERNMENT PRINTING OFFICE : 1966 O—224-230

83

Getting Stuck in the Basement

The basement fallout shelter, as described by Tom Vanderbilt in his book *Survival City: Adventures among the Ruins of Atomic America*, "was an admission that the traditional source of shelter—the home—was no longer sufficient *as it was*." Vanderbilt quotes the 1959 civil defense educational film *Walt Builds a Family Fallout Shelter*: "No home in America is modern without a family fallout shelter. This is the nuclear age."*Fallout shelters were considered an amenity for prospective home buyers, one that developers and real estate agents were always sure to advertise.

Vanderbilt discusses the "bright and shining architecture" of the period: "Glass-curtain walls, exuberant signage, out-sized picture windows, open-plan offices, sliding-glass patio doors and indoor/outdoor living, and drive-throughs." But there was, he added, "a brooding, subterranean fear" in a "parallel architecture of doom."

About civil defense pamphlets like this one, "Fallout Protection for Homes with Basements," and the one that follows it, "In Time of Emergency: A Citizen's Handbook on Nuclear Attack," Vanderbilt describes the "stiff, blank-stared homeowners lining their basements with sandbagged lean-tos." It was, he described, part of the civil defense effort "to depict the effects of nuclear attack without sending the populace into a state of passive paralysis."

Today's Federal Emergency Management Agency (FEMA) has taken up some of the efforts of the Office of Civil Defense. It took many decades for much of the outmoded planning to fall out of vogue, however. A 1980s FEMA survey looked at millions of buildings around the country for their fallout protection potential.

According to the *Philadelphia Inquirer*, the agency had "not been picky in choosing sites" among "office buildings, schools, supermarkets, churches, real estate offices—almost every public or semipublic building

---

* Leo A. Hoegh, director of the Office of Civil and Defense Mobilization, delivered a message at the end of *Walt Builds a Family Fallout Shelter* urging viewers to build shelters like Walt's: "In doing so, you not only protect your family, but you also contribute to the nation's security. You add to another strong deterrent to war."

with a basement." However, most fallout shelters in the blast zone, especially those built with the strain of concrete blocks attached to wooden joists as proposed in these government brochures, would cave in, according to modern civil defense experts. The *Inquirer* article pointed to a credibility gap in other "evacuation and shelter plans" that called for "120 people spending days or even weeks in the basement of the Kings Highway Inn [in Philadelphia]," describing them as "wildly optimistic."

Questions about the likelihood of getting out of a civilian shelter after an attack had been raised before. Vanderbilt quotes Robert Panero of the New York engineering firm Guy B. Panero discussing the "exit problem" in 1959: "If a military unit survives and operates during an attack period, it is not as important that the personnel operating the unit be capable of exiting; military people can be considered expendable. On the other hand, the civilian application . . . fails if the personnel or material cannot be removed after the attack or the war is over." Wildly optimistic, indeed.

This booklet has been specially prepared for householders whose basement has been analyzed by electronic computer for fallout protection as a result of a questionnaire which was filled out describing the house and basement.

Vote for Me—Or Get Blown Up

During the 2004 presidential campaign, Vice President Dick Cheney warned a town hall meeting in Des Moines, Iowa, about future terrorist attacks, saying, "It's absolutely essential that eight weeks from today, on November second, we make the right choice, because if we make the wrong choice then the danger is that we'll get hit again." This was not a new tactic in the political playbook.

Four decades earlier, Lyndon Johnson campaign spots frequently implied Barry Goldwater would rush to war with the Russkies. Pulling the lever for Goldwater would be like pushing the button, bringing down nuclear annihilation on the United States.

The most infamous example was the "Daisy" ad, aired just once by the Johnson campaign. It opened with a little girl in a field picking petals from a daisy. Her counting of the petals is replaced by a countdown and footage of a nuclear explosion. LBJ speaks over the mushroom

Democratic National Committee

cloud, saying, "These are the stakes! To make a world in which all of God's children can live, or to go into the dark. We must either love each other, or we must die."

A less provocative spot showed a little girl eating an ice cream cone while a voice-over explained the dangers of atomic bomb testing: "Children should have lots of vitamin A and calcium, but they shouldn't have any strontium-90 or caesium-137." Goldwater had been against a nuclear test ban treaty, the ad pointed out.

After LBJ crushed Goldwater in the 1964 election, his administration continued to support the building of private fallout shelters as a way of "saving millions of lives."

FALLOUT PROTECTION FOR HOMES WITH BASEMENTS

January 18, 1965

"It is already clear that without fallout shelter protection for our citizens, all defense weapons lose much of their effectiveness in saving lives. This also appears to be the least expensive way of saving millions of lives, and the one which has clear value even without other systems. We will continue our existing programs and start a program to increase the total inventory of shelters through a survey of private home and other small structures."

President of United States

Excerpt from the President's message to the Congress

THE FALLOUT PROTECTION IN YOUR HOME

This booklet is about fallout protection. It will tell you what radioactive fallout is and how you can improve your protection against it if this country were ever attacked with nuclear weapons. But first of all, because your home has a basement, you already have some fallout protection. Let's see what that protection is:

The back cover of this booklet looks something like this:

Occupant
1234 Main Street
Washington, D. C. 20005

BASEMENT PF (PROTECTION FACTOR)		ADDED WEIGHT
CENTER	BEST CORNER	

Your own address is on the back cover of your booklet. Entered in the box labeled Basement "PF" are two numbers which tell you the fallout protection that was calculated for the "center" of your basement and the "best corner" of your basement. These numbers are based on the best engineering and scientific knowledge available. Information on the box labeled "Added Weight", is on page 20 of this booklet.

The "PF" above the box stands for "Protection Factor." Before going into the details of what your "Protection Factor" numbers mean, let's talk for a moment about what fallout is.

WHAT IS RADIOACTIVE FALLOUT?

When a nuclear weapon is exploded close to the ground, dirt and other debris are drawn up into the mushroom cloud and pick up the radioactivity created by the explosion. The heaviest pieces of dirt and debris drop back to earth within a few miles of the explosion. But the lighter pieces are carried by the winds for many miles before drifting back to earth.

These radioactive particles are called "fallout." Any part of the United States might be covered with deadly or dangerous amounts of radioactive fallout, depending on which way the winds were blowing and the size and number of nuclear weapons exploded. The radioactivity could cause serious health damage or fatal injury to unprotected persons. In a nuclear attack, the

3

blast, heat, and fire from the explosions would be very destructive, but the destruction would be in the areas near the explosions. Radioactive fallout, though, could spread in a thin layer over millions of square miles.

Radiation would come from the fallout wherever it settled—the ground, trees and bushes, or the roof of your home. *Fallout does not behave like a gas.* In areas that would be affected by dangerous amounts of fallout, the fallout particles would look like dirt or sand and you may see them after they have settled on the ground or other places. The exact amount of radiation given off by the particles can be measured only by special instruments.

HOW CAN YOUR PROTECTION BE IMPROVED?

There are three ways of improving your protection against fallout—time, distance, and getting some heavy material between you and the fallout (called "shielding").

1. *Time*—Radioactivity decreases rapidly at first. After an attack, the radiation would be most intense during the first few days. Even so, radiation protection may be needed for an extended period—days or weeks.

2. *Distance*—The amount of radiation is less the further away you are from the source of radiation.

3. *Shielding*—Any material that is put between a person and the source of radiation cuts down the amount of radiation that reaches the person. The thicker and heavier the material, the better the protection.

In the event of an attack, you have little control over time and distance, but YOU CAN DO SOMETHING TO IMPROVE YOUR PROTECTION BY MEANS OF SHIELDING.

It is the principle of shielding that is employed in fallout shelters. Under the guidance of the Office of Civil Defense, a system of fallout shelters is being developed throughout the nation. It consists of public shelters, private shelters, industrial and home shelters.

4

THE FALLOUT SHELTER SYSTEM

As a result of the National Fallout Shelter Survey, in which existing large buildings were examined and evaluated for fallout protection, space for millions of people has been identified. Those community shelters having a protection factor of at least 40 and space for at least 50 people are now being marked with the familiar black and yellow shelter sign. Where necessary storage space is available, they are being stocked with food, water (if needed), sanitary and medical supplies, and radiation detection instruments. The survey is a continuing effort. Through it, a current inventory is maintained of shelters added by new construction.

The fallout protection found in homes with basements represents important additional shelter space.

Personal and other special considerations may make fallout protection at home more practical or desirable than community shelters for certain individuals or families. For example, in rural and suburban communities and even in many cities, families may live a considerable distance from the nearest community shelter. For these families, a home shelter will provide more accessible fallout protection. Fallout protection at home is usually more accessible to housewives and young children during the day and may be preferred by the whole family when at home.

HOW MUCH PROTECTION DOES YOUR BASEMENT PROVIDE AGAINST RADIOACTIVE FALLOUT?

In homes, basement areas provide the best shelter against fallout because they are mostly belowground. This gives them a natural shield. This booklet tells you the amount of protection your basement offers and what you can do to increase this protection to provide for your family's safety. Keep in mind that fallout shelter provides only limited protection against blast.

Look at the back of this booklet again. Two numbers are printed there which tell you the amount of fallout protection your basement offers. These numbers were calculated for your home from the information you gave in the recent questionnaire on Evaluation of Fallout Protection in Homes.

The numbers are given in terms of a "Protection Factor" or PF. This is the relation between the amount of fallout radiation

5

which would be received by a completely unprotected person compared to the amount which would be received by a person in a fallout shelter. For example, a person in a fallout shelter with a PF of 40 would receive about one-fortieth (or 2½ percent) of the radiation he would be exposed to if he were completely unprotected. The higher the PF for your home, the more protection your basement affords against radiation.

BASEMENT PF (PROTECTION FACTOR)		ADDED WEIGHT
CENTER	BEST CORNER	

The number in the box marked "center" (see back of your booklet) is the Basement Protection Factor (PF) calculated for the center of your basement. The other number is the PF calculated for the best corner of your basement. If your cover shows an X in place of either PF number, it means the PF is smaller than 10. Information on the box labeled "Added Weight," is on page 20 of this booklet.

WHICH IS THE BEST CORNER OF YOUR BASEMENT?

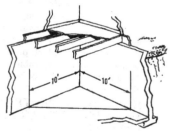

The best corner of your basement is the one which has the highest outside ground level— that is, the least amount of basement wall sticking up aboveground. In this corner make a triangle by measuring ten feet from the corner along each wall, and drawing a line between these points (see illustration).

The best corner protection factor listed on the back of this booklet means the average protection factor within the triangle is above this value. This 50 sq. ft. area provides adequate fallout shelter space for 5 persons. However, if necessary, several more persons could crowd into the corner area.

A smaller area could be used if equipment such as a furnace occupies part of the corner. If additional shelter space is required or the best corner is not usable, another corner having the next highest ground level to that of the best corner could be used. If all the corners have equal outside ground levels, the most convenient corner may be used, and of course all corners may be used.

6

The fallout protection afforded in the corner is better closer to the wall and closer to the floor. Therefore, you should lie on the floor next to the wall or sit on the floor with your back against the wall as much as possible. You may stand to stretch, and for essential needs, you can leave the corner shelter area for a few minutes.

WHAT ABOUT THE CENTER OF THE BASEMENT?

In nearly all basements, the highest protection factor is in the corner and the lowest is in the center. This means the whole basement can be thought of as a fallout shelter with a protection factor in the center equal to the first PF number on the back of your booklet and a higher protection factor in the best corner equal to the second PF number.

STEPS YOU CAN TAKE TO INCREASE YOUR FALLOUT PROTECTION

If the protection factor in the best corner of your basement as indicated on the back cover is less than 40 and you wish to bring the PF up to the minimum recommended for public shelter, then you need additional shielding.

You can provide additional shielding for your basement by:

1. *Permanent shelters*—By making part of your basement into a shelter area or by building a permanent shelter which might also serve other purposes. Listed on the back label are the plans recommended for your home.

2. *Preplanned shelters*—By locating shielding materials so that you can complete a shelter quickly in time of crisis.

3. *Improvised shelters*—By taking last-minute improvised actions if an emergency actually occurs.

A WORD OF CAUTION TO THE HOME HANDY MAN

Fallout Shelter Plans A through F which follow are so simple that you may be tempted to construct them from the drawings in this booklet—and in many cases a thoroughly experienced "do-it-yourselfer" could do this. However, it requires very careful calculation of materials and fasteners to safely hold the heavy materials to be placed overhead; therefore, it is strongly recommended that you build from the detailed plans and lists of materials which are available by mailing the post card enclosed with this booklet.

7

PERMANENT SHELTER

Ceiling Modification To Basement   PLAN A

NOTE: If too much of the basement wall is exposed, this plan will not provide sufficient protection and should not be used. The back cover of this booklet will indicate if this plan is recommended for <u>YOUR</u> home.

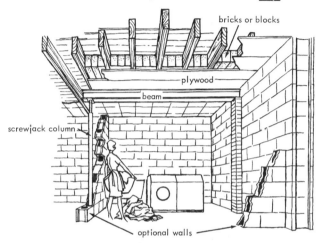

bricks or blocks

plywood

beam

screwjack column

optional walls

Here is a shelter which can be permanently installed in the basement of your home without affecting the use of the basement in any way.

All that is needed is a basement, some basic woodworking skills and approximately $165 for materials.   The shelter can be accomplished while the basement is being built or it can be added to an existing basement by modifying the ceiling in the corner which furnishes the best protection.

A significant amount of protection can be achieved merely by inserting heavy material in the ceiling above the best corner if this plan is recommended for your home.   If this plan is not indicated on the back cover of your booklet, it can still be used by providing two additional masonry walls to enclose the corner of the basement.   Fixtures and installation of ceiling tiles or walls will increase the cost a bit, but you will be able to achieve a significant amount of protection without interfering with the functions of the basement.

8

Because the basement area is almost all belowground level, you can increase the fallout protection by installing bricks or solid concrete blocks between the wood joists in the best corner. The filler materials are supported by sheets of plywood fastened to the floor joists. A beam and screw jack column may be needed to keep the floor joists from bending too much. A carpenter can tell you if this is needed.

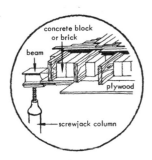

Plywood sheets (2' x 8' x ½" cut to fit) should be securely fastened to the joists using 2 inch, #8 screws 10 inches apart. Bricks or blocks are then packed as tightly as possible into the openings between the joists. Be sure to fill as much space as possible. To get the most protection out of this improvement, one-quarter of the basement ceiling over the best corner should be filled with bricks or solid concrete blocks.

To obtain detailed plans, see page 24.

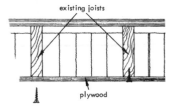

In fastening the plywood sheets to the joists, nailing is not enough. Nails will pull loose. Use two-inch screws in the manner shown here.

9

PERMANENT SHELTER

Alternate Ceiling Modification To Basement   PLAN B

NOTE: If too much of the basement wall is exposed, this plan will not provide sufficient protection and should not be used. The back cover of this booklet will indicate if this plan is recommended for **YOUR** home.

If you need a minimum shelter which will not interfere with an existing corner of your basement, try this plan. It is so arranged that the shelter area can be enlarged at either end, depending upon the size of the basement.

This type of construction does not require a beam and screw-jack column to support the joists. The protected area can be used as a workshop, recreation room, pantry area, laundry room, or part of a family room. With ceiling tile covering the plywood panels, no one would recognize the area as a fallout shelter. Since the objective is to provide as much overhead mass as possible, the heaviest weight of solid brick or block (placed on an end if possible) should be used. If this plan is not indicated on the back cover of this booklet, it can still be used by providing two additional masonry walls to enclose the corner of the basement.

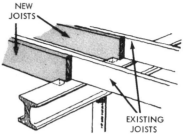

Wooden joists (2" x 12"), notched at the ends for bearing, are installed between existing floor joists. Plywood panels are then fastened to the 2" x 12" joists.

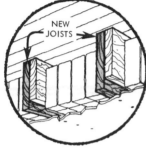

Brick or concrete blocks are packed into the spaces between the 10" and 12" joists; they are supported by the plywood panels.

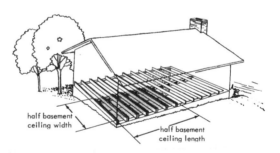

half basement ceiling width

half basement ceiling length

This basement floor plan shows how the additional joists and the filler material might be used in the corner of the basement which furnishes the best fallout protection. To get the most protection out of this improvement, one-quarter of the basement ceiling should be filled with bricks or solid concrete blocks.

To obtain detailed plans, See page 24.

11

PERMANENT SHELTER

Concrete Block Shelter   PLAN C (for best corner of basement)

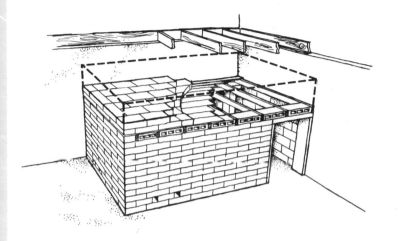

The above concrete block shelter is designed to provide a protection factor of at least 40 when placed in the basement.   Its principal advantages are simple design, speed of construction and ready availability of low-cost materials.   It can be designed as a sit-down shelter, or by increasing the ceiling height to 6 feet or more, it could make a more comfortable shelter and serve a dual purpose as a storage room or similar facility.   The shelter ceiling, however, should not be higher than the outside ground level in the basement corner where the shelter is located.   The ground level could be raised as shown on pages 18 and 19.

Natural ventilation is provided by the entrance and the air vents in the shelter wall.   Materials for this type of shelter will cost an estimated $135–$150 depending on its height and the area of the country.

To obtain detailed plans, see page 24.

12

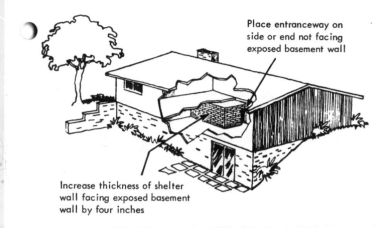

Place entranceway on side or end not facing exposed basement wall

Increase thickness of shelter wall facing exposed basement wall by four inches

If your basement ceiling is near ground level on three sides and exposed on one side (as with "walk-in" basements), the concrete block shelter (Plan C) must be modified to achieve the desired effectiveness. The following changes should be made:

1. Increase the thickness of the shelter wall facing the basement wall which has no ground cover by four inches of brick, concrete block or similar materials.

2. Place the shelter entrance on a side or end which does *not* face the exposed basement wall.

13

PRE-PLANNED SHELTERS

Snack Bar   PLAN D (for best corner of basement)

A snack bar built of brick or block can be converted into a fallout shelter in a short period of time by lowering a strong hinged false ceiling to rest on the snack bar.

The false ceiling section can then be loaded with brick or block. The bricks or blocks can be conveniently stored by incorporating them into recreation room furniture such as benches and room dividers.

An attractive bench unit for your recreation room can be made from blocks or brick. Pillows and a wood frame to enclose the bench will provide a finishing touch.

To obtain detailed plans, See page 24.

14

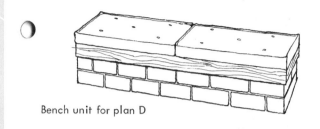

Bench unit for plan D

Tilt-Up Storage Unit   PLAN E   (for best corner of basement)

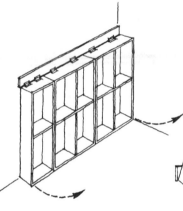

A tilt-up storage unit in a corner of your basement is another approach similar to the snack bar. The top of the storage unit can be hinged to the wall and the unit can be used as a bookcase, pantry shelves, or for miscellaneous storage.

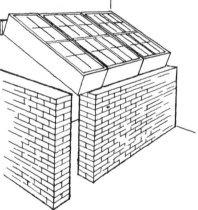

In an emergency, the storage unit can be tilted so that it rests on a wall of brick or concrete blocks stored for just such as emergency. Additional bricks or blocks can then be placed in the storage unit to provide an overhead shield.

To obtain detailed plans, see page 24.

15

PRE-PLANNED SHELTERS

Lean-To Shelter   PLAN F   (for best corner of basement)

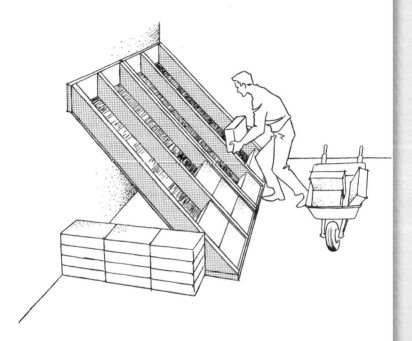

A simple and effective lean-to shelter can be built by constructing the components and storing them in your basement where they can be quickly assembled in an emergency. Components consist of a frame and filler materials, such as brick or blocks.

For detailed plans, see page 24.

16

A patio of brick or concrete block supported on a bed of sand will provide a ready source of shielding material which could be quickly removed for use in an emergency. See Plans D, E and F.

Enclosing your patio area with a solid masonry screen wall will give you privacy for lounging and cook-outs, and will provide a barrier shield to increase the PF in the basement area.

17

AN ELEVATED FLOWER GARDEN

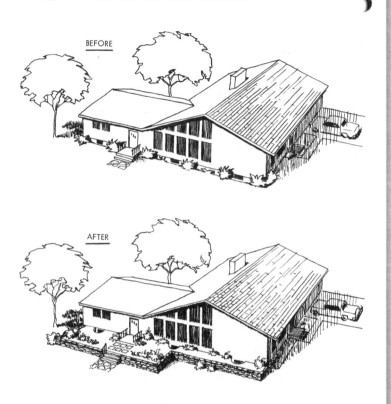

Where basements are not completely belowgrade, here are some additional ideas which can be used to increase the shielding of exposed basement walls. A brick, masonry, or stone planter box along one or more sides of the house will improve protection substantially, and will provide an attractive setting for shrubs and flowers as well. If the partially exposed wall is at the rear or side of the house, an elevated garden could be built with masonry retaining walls.

18

If the partially exposed walls have windows, these can still be used by providing window wells within the planter box or elevated garden area.

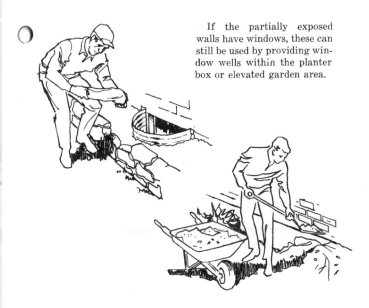

Your basement's PF will also be increased by providing additional shielding to the exposed section. This can be done by piling patio block, sand, earth, cordwood or similar materials against the exposed wall.

19

IMPROVISED SHELTERS

If a community shelter is not available and you have not provided your own fallout shelter, what would you do if you suddenly heard that the United States had been attacked with nuclear weapons?

You can still protect yourself and your family if you know what to do and if you act quickly. Pick out the corner of your basement with the highest ground level outside. That is the safest place in the basement. **NOW MAKE IT SAFER.**

In belowground basements, it is most important to have shielding overhead. Entered in the box labeled "Added Weight" on the back cover of this booklet is a number which tells you approximately how much weight of material should be placed over each square foot of the area over an improvised shelter, as illustrated on the following pages, to obtain a PF of 40, the minimum recommended.

If the letter "Y" appears in the box labeled "Added Weight" this means that adding overhead materials alone will not provide adequate protection against radiation unless heavy walls surrounding the shelter area are also added. If you already have a PF of 40 or more in the best corner of your basement, a zero, "0," will be shown in the box on the back cover labeled "Added Weight" indicating that additional weight is not required.

BASEMENT PF (PROTECTION FACTOR)		ADDED WEIGHT
CENTER	BEST CORNER	
·		

YOUR OWN NUMBER WILL APPEAR IN THIS BOX
ON THE BACK COVER OF THIS BOOKLET.

Here are the weights of typical shielding materials:

4 inches of sand weighs approx. **35 pounds per sq. ft.**

4 inches of wood weighs approx. **10 pounds per sq. ft.**

4 inches of water weighs approx. **21 pounds per sq. ft.**

4-inch cinder blocks weigh approx. **22 pounds per sq. ft.**

4-inch bricks weigh approx. **32 pounds per sq. ft.**

4-inch solid concrete blocks weigh approx. **48 pounds per sq. ft.**

4 inches of library books weigh approx. **15 pounds per sq. ft.**

20

If you have a sturdy table or workbench, place it in the corner. Quickly fill drawers or boxes with the heaviest material which is readily available—sand or dirt, bricks—or if you have nothing heavier, newspapers or books.   Stack these materials on the top of the workbench.   If a "Y" appears in the "Added Weight" box on the back cover of this booklet, then in order to obtain a PF of 40 in the shelter you must place an equivalent of 70 pounds per square foot on top of the shelter *as well* as adding heavy material on the sides of the shelter.

Be careful not to overload the table to the point where it will collapse.

21

IMPROVISED SHELTERS

If a workbench is not available, you can improvise a somewhat larger shelter area by using furniture, doors, dressers, or other materials. Remove doors from their hinges and place them over supports in the corner of your basement having the best protection. The supports for the table can be chests of drawers or anything that can take a heavy load. Use two or three doors over each support for this shelter to provide sufficient strength to carry the heavy loads placed on them. Place bricks, concrete blocks, earth- or sand-filled drawers, books, a collapsible children's swimming pool filled with water, etc., over the doors to provide an overhead shield. Use anything with weight that can be moved. The heavier the material, the more the protection. The minimum weight of material to be added for each square foot over the doors is shown in the "Added Weight" box on the back cover. If a "Y" appears in the "Added Weight" box, then in order to obtain a PF of 40 in the shelter, you must place 70 pounds per square foot on top of the shelter *as well* as adding heavy material to the sides of the shelter to serve as a vertical shield.

Be careful not to overload the doors to the point where the shelter will collapse.

22

If the figure entered in the box marked "Added Weight" on the back cover happens to be a number such as 30, this means that *every square foot* over the shelter area should be covered with material having a sufficient height so as to weigh 30 pounds. Using the weights of typical shielding materials as given on page 20, the required shielding material can be obtained by the following:

> Approximately 3½ inches of earth or sand or
>
> Approximately 12 inches of wood or
>
> Approximately 6 inches of water or
>
> 4-inch (nominal thickness) layer of bricks or
>
> Approximately 8 inches of library books

The shielding materials can be used individually such as providing a 3½-inch layer of sand completely over the improvised shelter or in conjunction with other materials as shown in the illustration on the opposite page.

If vertical shielding is required (a "Y" has appeared in the "Added Weight" box) this can be obtained by placing heavy material along the sides of the improvised shelter. Examples are: single course of bricks or concrete blocks, washing machine filled with water, chest of drawers filled with earth, deep-freeze, two rows of books, etc.

GENERAL

Until the extent of the radiation threat in your town is determined by trained monitors using special instruments, you should stay in your shelter as much as possible. For essential needs, you can leave your shelter for a few minutes. Before leaving the shelter for longer periods of time, listen to your radio station for information and instructions. A battery operated radio should be available for this purpose.

For quick reference, after you have finished reading this booklet, hang it up in the corner of your basement having the best protection so that it will be available in an emergency.

23

DETAILED PLANS ARE AVAILABLE FREE OF CHARGE

Detailed plans of many of the shelters you have read about in this booklet are available free of charge.

These plans contain construction details, suggested construction sequences and lists of materials needed. The plans supplement the material presented in this booklet.

Before constructing any of the permanent shielding devices described here, you should check to see that the construction conforms to your local building code.

The plans may be obtained by sending the attached post card to the Jeffersonville Census Operations Office, 1201 East 10th Street, Jeffersonville, Indiana 47130

Be sure that you identify the plan or plans you want as they are designated in the booklet:

PLAN A — CEILING MODIFICATION TO
        BASEMENT   — See page 8

PLAN B — ALTERNATE CEILING MODIFI-
        CATION TO BASEMENT   — See page 10

PLAN C — CONCRETE BLOCK SHELTER   — See page 12

PLAN D — SNACK BAR SHELTER   — See page 14

PLAN E — TILT-UP STORAGE UNIT   — See page 15

PLAN F — LEAN-TO SHELTER   — See page 16

For further information on fallout protection and personal and family survival, consult your local Civil Defense Director and send for the personal and family survival booklet using the attached post card.

☆ U.S. GOVERNMENT PRINTING OFFICE : 1966 O—237-813

Jeffersonville Census Operations Office
1201 East 10th Street
Jeffersonville, Indiana   47130

PLEASE SEND ME DETAILED PLANS FOR THE FOLLOWING
FALLOUT SHELTERS (CHECK BOX FOR DESIRED PLAN)

☐ PLAN A — Ceiling Modification to Basement

☐ PLAN B — Alternate Ceiling Modification to Basement

☐ PLAN C — Concrete Block Shelter

☐ PLAN D — Snack Bar Shelter

☐ PLAN E — Tilt-up Storage Unit

☐ PLAN F — Lean-to Shelter

☐ Personal and Family Survival Booklet

Insert your label number found
above your address on the
back of the Fallout Book

Label No. [| | | | | |]

Name _____

Street or Box No. _____

City and State _____ Zip Code _____

Handy prepaid postcard (front and back) included with *Fallout Protection for Homes with Basements*, to be used for ordering free shelter construction plans. This family's mailing label (opposite) indicates they could have chosen from plans C through F—including the ever popular Snack Bar Shelter.

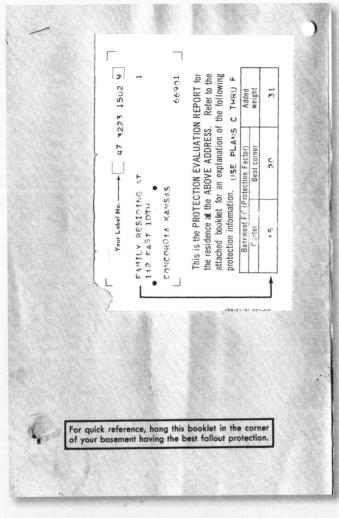

Your Label No. ⟶ 47 7223 1502 9

1

FAMILY RESIDING AT
112 EAST 10TH
CONCORDIA KANSAS

66901

This is the PROTECTION EVALUATION REPORT for the residence at the ABOVE ADDRESS. Refer to the attached booklet for an explanation of the following protection information. USE PLANS C THRU F

Basement PF (Protection Factor)		Added weight
Center	Best corner	
15	20	31

For quick reference, hang this booklet in the corner of your basement having the best fallout protection.

The personalized mailing label shows a Basement Protection Factor (PF) of 20 in the best corner, half of the minimum recommended PF of 40. The Added Weight figure indicates the family has to add thirty-one pounds of overhead shielding per square foot of ceiling above the shelter to achieve a PF 40 rating. Filling the shelter's ceiling with four inches of sand would take care of it.

The "spray dome" formed over the point of burst in a shallow underwater explosion.
United States Atomic Energy Commission

The condensation cloud formed after a shallow underwater explosion. (The "slick," due to the shock wave, can be seen on the water's surface.) *United States Atomic Energy Commission*

Formation of the hollow column in a shallow underwater explosion, with the top surrounded by a late stage of the condensation cloud. *United States Atomic Energy Commission*

The radioactive cloud and first stages of the base surge following a shallow underwater burst. Water is beginning to fall back from the column into the lagoon. *United States Atomic Energy Commission*

The development of the base surge following a shallow underwater explosion. *United States Atomic Energy Commission*

Final stage in the development of the base surge. *United States Atomic Energy Commission*

Reinforced Shelters, Reinforced Gender Roles

According to a 1986 *Chicago Tribune* article, critics like Robert Sachs, a physicist who headed the Enrico Fermi Institute at the University of Chicago, "object to the boosterism they see implied" in civil defense handouts like those above "that show people calmly waiting out a holocaust in the relative comfort of a basement fallout shelter." Sachs calls it delusional "that there's a practical defense to nuclear war," scoffing at the notion that people would "just stay down in your shelter and lay in your supply of videocassette tapes."

"Nuclear Families: The Home Fallout Shelter Movement in California, 1950–1969," was a 2002 museum exhibition curated by Elizabeth Kathleen Mitchell. The *Los Angeles Times* asked Mitchell to explain the rise of "shelter mentality" during the period, which the article described as "pitting neighbor against neighbor when homeowners considered who they'd take underground, and who they'd leave behind."

To Mitchell, the mentality reinforced rigid gender roles, "mother as nurturer and father as builder and protector," according to the article. Mitchell pointed to "an illustrated poster with 'Protect Them!' in large type" that depicted "a quintessential 1950s-era mother comforting her cowering children." Mitchell opined, "It was obviously directed at the father, who was in charge of protecting his family. . . . The government was telling you how to behave. . . . Everybody had to know their role, or they'd die."

IN TIME OF EMERGENCY

A Citizen's Handbook on Nuclear Attack

MARCH 1968

DEPARTMENT OF DEFENSE

Office of Civil Defense

UNDERSTAND THE HAZARDS OF NUCLEAR ATTACK

When a nuclear bomb or missile explodes, the main effects produced are intense light (flash), heat, blast, and radiation. How strong these effects are depends on the size and type of the weapon; how far away the explosion is; the weather conditions (sunny or rainy, windy or still); the terrain (whether the ground is flat or hilly); and the height of the explosion (high in the air, or near the ground).

All nuclear explosions cause light, heat and blast, which occur immediately. In addition, explosions that are on or close to the ground would create large quantities of dangerous radioactive fallout particles, most of which would fall to earth during the first 24 hours. Explosions high in the air would create smaller radioactive particles, which would not have any real effect on humans until many months or years later, if at all.*

What Would Happen in an Enemy Attack

If the U.S. should be attacked, the people who happened to be close to a nuclear explosion—in the area of heavy destruction—probably would be killed or seriously injured by the blast, or by the heat of the nuclear fireball.

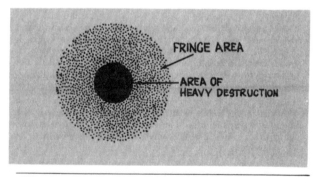

FRINGE AREA

AREA OF HEAVY DESTRUCTION

---

*These smaller particles would drift to earth more slowly, losing much of their radioactivity before they reached the ground, and would be spread by the upper winds over vast areas of the world.

People a few miles away—in the "fringe area" of the explosion—would be endangered by the blast and heat, and by fires that the explosion might start. However, it is likely that most of the people in the fringe area would survive these hazards.

People who were *outside* the fringe area would not be affected by the blast, heat or fire. Department of Defense studies show that in any nuclear attack an enemy might launch against us, tens of millions of Americans would be outside the fringe areas. To them—and to people in the fringe areas who survived the blast, heat and fire—radioactive fallout would be the main danger. Protective measures against this danger can be taken.

What Is Fallout?

When a nuclear weapon explodes near the ground, great quantities of pulverized earth and other debris are sucked up into the nuclear cloud. There the radioactive gases produced by the explosion condense on and into this debris, producing radioactive fallout particles. Within a short time, these particles fall back to earth—the larger ones first, the smaller ones later. On the way down, and after they reach the ground, the radioactive particles give off invisible gamma rays—like X-rays—too much of which can kill or injure people. These particles give off most of their radiation quickly; therefore the first few hours or days after an attack would be the most dangerous period.

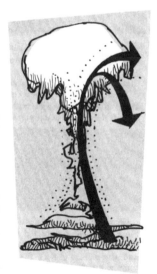

11

In dangerously affected areas the particles themselves would look like grains of salt or sand; but the *rays* they would give off could not be seen, tasted, smelled or felt. Special instruments would be required to detect the rays and measure their intensity.

Fallout Would Be Widespread

The distribution of fallout particles after a nuclear attack would depend on wind currents, weather conditions and other factors. There is no way of predicting in advance what areas of the country would be affected by fallout, or how soon the particles would fall back to earth at a particular location.

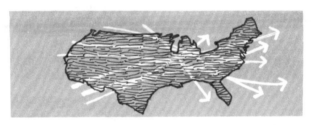

Some communities might get a heavy accumulation of fallout, while others—even in the same general area—might get little or none. No area in the U.S. could be sure of *not* getting fallout, and it is probable that some fallout particles would be deposited on most of the country.

Areas close to a nuclear explosion might receive fallout within 15–30 minutes. It might take 5–10 hours or more for the particles to drift down on a community 100 or 200 miles away.

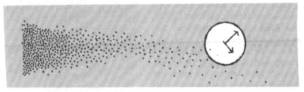

Generally, the first 24 hours after fallout began to settle would be the most dangerous period to a community's residents. The heavier particles falling during that time would still be highly radioactive and give off strong rays. The lighter particles falling later would have lost much of their radiation high in the atmosphere.

12

Fallout Causes Radiation Sickness

The invisible gamma rays given off by fallout particles can cause radiation sickness—that is, illness caused by physical and chemical changes in the cells of the body. If a person receives a large dose of radiation, he will die. But if he receives only a small or medium dose, his body will repair itself and he will get well. The same dose received over a short period of time is more damaging than if it is received over a longer period. Usually, the effects of a given dose of radiation are more severe in very young and very old persons, and those not in good health.

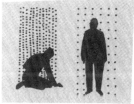

No special clothing can protect people against gamma radiation, and no special drugs or chemicals can prevent large doses of radiation from causing damage to the cells of the body. However, antibiotics and other medicines are helpful in treating infections that sometimes follow excessive exposure to radiation (which weakens the body's ability to fight infections).

Almost all of the radiation that people would absorb from fallout particles would come from particles *outside* their own bodies. Only simple precautions would be necessary to avoid swallowing the particles, and because of their size (like grains of sand) it would be practically impossible to inhale them.

People exposed to fallout radiation do *not* become radioactive and thereby dangerous to other people. Radiation sickness is not contagious or infectious, and one person cannot "catch it" from another person.

Protection Is Possible

People can protect themselves against fallout radiation, and have a good chance of surviving it, by staying inside a fallout shelter. In most cases, the fallout radiation level outside the shelter would decrease rapidly enough to permit people to leave the shelter within a few days.

Even in communities that received heavy accumulations of fallout particles, people soon might be able to leave shelter for a few minutes or a few hours at a time in order to perform emergency tasks. In most places, it is unlikely that full-time shelter occupancy would be required for more than a week or two.

13

Many Kinds of Fallout Shelters

The farther away you are from the fallout particles outside, the less radiation you will receive. Also, the building materials (concrete, brick, lumber, etc.) that are between you and the fallout particles serve to absorb many of the gamma rays and keep them from reaching you.

A fallout shelter, therefore, does not need to be a special type of building or an underground bunker. It can be *any space*, provided the walls and roof are thick or heavy enough to absorb many of the rays given off by the fallout particles outside, and thus keep dangerous amounts of radiation from reaching the people inside the structure.

A shelter can be the basement or inner corridor of any large building; the basement of a private home; a subway or tunnel; or even a backyard trench with some kind of shielding material (heavy lumber, earth, bricks, etc.) serving as a roof.

In addition to protecting people from fallout radiation, most fallout shelters also would provide some limited protection against the blast and heat effects of nuclear explosions that were not close by.

Chapter 4 (pages 23–32) discusses the various types of fallout shelters that people can use to protect themselves in case of nuclear attack.

Food and Water Would Be Available and Usable

From many studies, the Federal Government has determined that enough food and water would be available after an attack to sustain our surviving citizens. However, temporary food shortages might occur in some areas, until food was shipped there from other areas.

14

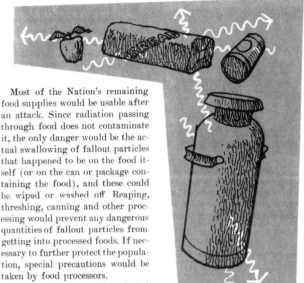

Most of the Nation's remaining food supplies would be usable after an attack. Since radiation passing through food does not contaminate it, the only danger would be the actual swallowing of fallout particles that happened to be on the food itself (or on the can or package containing the food), and these could be wiped or washed off. Reaping, threshing, canning and other processing would prevent any dangerous quantities of fallout particles from getting into processed foods. If necessary to further protect the population, special precautions would be taken by food processors.

Water systems might be affected somewhat by radioactive fallout, but the risk would be small, especially if a few simple precautions were taken. Water stored in covered containers and water in covered wells would not be contaminated after an attack, because the fallout particles could not get into the water. Even if the containers were not covered (such as buckets or bathtubs filled with emergency supplies of water), as long as they were indoors it is highly unlikely that fallout particles would get into them.

Practically all of the particles that dropped into open reservoirs, lakes, and streams (or into open containers or wells) would settle to the bottom. Any that didn't would be removed when the water was filtered before being pumped to consumers. A small amount of radioactive material might dissolve in the water, but at most this would be of concern for only a few weeks.

15

Milk contamination from fallout is not expected to be a serious problem after an attack. If cows graze on contaminated pasture and swallow fallout particles that contain some radioactive elements, their milk might be harmful to the thyroid glands of infants and small children. Therefore, if possible, they should be given canned or powdered milk for a few weeks if authorities say the regular milk supply is contaminated by radioactive elements.

In summary, the danger of people receiving harmful doses of fallout radiation through food, water or milk is very small. People suffering from extreme hunger or thirst should not be denied these necessities after an attack, even if the only available supplies might contain fallout particles or other radioactive substances.

16

KNOW ABOUT WARNING

An enemy attack on the United States probably would be preceded by a period of international tension or crisis. This crisis period would help alert all citizens to the *possibility* of attack.

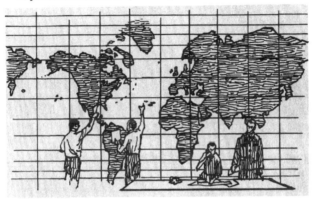

If an attack actually occurs, it is almost certain that incoming enemy planes and missiles would be detected by our networks of warning stations in time for citizens to get into shelters or at least take cover. This warning time might be as little as 5–15 minutes in some locations, or as much as an hour or more in others.

How you received warning of an attack would depend on where you happened to be at that time. You might hear the warning given on radio or television, or even by word-of-mouth. Or your first notice of attack might come from the outdoor warning system in your own city, town or village.

Many U.S. cities and towns have outdoor warning systems, using sirens, whistles, horns or bells. Although they have been installed mainly to warn citizens of enemy attack, some local governments also use them in connection with natural disasters and other peacetime catastrophes.

Different cities and towns are using their outdoor warning systems in different ways. Most local governments, however, have decided to use a certain signal to warn people of an enemy attack, and a different signal to notify them of a peacetime disaster.

18

The Standard Warning Signals

The two "standard" signals that have been adopted in *most* communities are these:

THE ATTACK WARNING SIGNAL. This will be sounded only in case of enemy attack. The signal itself is a 3- to 5-minute *wavering sound* on the sirens, or a *series of short blasts* on whistles, horns or other devices, repeated as deemed necessary. The Attack Warning

Signal means that an actual enemy attack against the United States has been detected, and that protective action should be taken immediately. This signal has no other meaning, and will be used for no other purpose.

THE ATTENTION OR ALERT SIGNAL. This is used by some local governments to get the attention of citizens in a time of threatened or impending natural disaster, or some other peacetime emergency. The signal itself is a 3- to 5-minute *steady blast* on sirens,

whistles, horns or other devices. In most places, the Attention or Alert Signal means that the local government wants to broadcast important information on radio or television concerning a peacetime disaster. (See Chapter 1 of Major Natural Disasters section of this handbook.)

What To Do When Signals Sound

1. *If you should hear the Attack Warning Signal*—unless your local government has instructed you otherwise—go immediately to a public fallout shelter marked like this, or to your home fallout shelter. Turn on a radio, tune it to any local station that is broadcasting, and listen

for official information. Follow whatever instructions are given.

If you are at home and there is no public or private shelter available, you may be able to improvise some last-minute protection for yourself and your family by following the suggestions in Chapter 5 (pages 33–38) of this handbook. As a last resort, take cover anywhere you can.

2. If you should hear the Attention or Alert Signal, turn on a radio or TV set, tune it to any local station, and follow the official instructions being broadcast.

Don't Use the Telephone

Whichever signal is sounding, *don't* use the telephone to obtain further information and advice about the emergency. Depend on the radio or television, since the government will be broadcasting all the information it has available. The telephone lines will be needed for official calls. Help keep them open.

Learn Your Community's Signals Now

As mentioned before not all communities in the U.S. have outdoor warning systems, and not all communities with warning systems have adopted the two "standard" warning signals.

You should therefore *find out now* from your local Civil Defense Office what signals are being used. in *your* community; what they sound like; what they mean; and what actions you should take when you hear them. Then memorize this information, or write it down on a card to carry with you at all times. Also, post it in your home. Check at least once each year to see if there are any changes.

If There Is a Nuclear Flash

It is possible—but extremely unlikely—that your first warning of an enemy attack might be the flash of a nuclear explosion in the sky some distance away. Or there might be a flash after warning had been given, possibly while you were on your way to shelter.

● TAKE COVER INSTANTLY. If there should be a nuclear flash—especially if you are outdoors and feel warmth at the same time—take cover *instantly* in the best place you can find. By getting inside or under something within a few *seconds*, you might avoid being seriously burned by the heat or injured by the blast wave of the nuclear explosion. If the explosion were some distance away, you might have 5 to 15 *seconds* before being seriously injured by the heat, and perhaps 30 to 60 *seconds* before the blast wave arrived. Getting under cover within these time limits might save your life or avoid serious injury. Also, to avoid injuring your eyes, *never look at the flash of an explosion or the nuclear fireball.*

21

● WHERE TO TAKE COVER.

You could take cover in any kind of a building, a storm cellar or fruit cellar, a subway station or tunnel— or even in a ditch or culvert alongside the road, a highway underpass, a storm sewer, a cave or outcropping of rock, a pile of heavy materials, a trench or other excavation. Even getting under a parked automobile, bus or train, or a heavy piece of furniture, would protect you to some extent. If no cover is available, simply lie down on the ground and curl up. The important thing is to avoid being burned by the heat, thrown about by the blast, or struck by flying objects.

● BEST POSITION AFTER TAKING COVER.

After taking cover you should lie on your side in a curled-up position, and cover your head with your arms and hands. This would give you some additional protection.

● MOVE TO A FALLOUT SHELTER LATER.

If you protected yourself against the blast and heat waves by instantly taking cover, you could get protection from the radioactive fallout (which would arrive later) by moving to a fallout shelter.

22

FALLOUT SHELTERS, PUBLIC AND PRIVATE

After a nuclear attack, fallout particles would drift down on most areas of this country. To protect themselves from the radiation given off by these particles, people in affected areas would have to stay in fallout shelters for 2 or 3 days to as long as 2 weeks. Many people would go to public fallout shelters, while others—through choice or necessity—would take refuge in private or home fallout shelters.

Identifying Public Shelters

Most communities now have public fallout shelters that would protect many of their residents against fallout radiation. Where there are still not enough public shelters to accommodate all citizens, efforts are being made to provide more. In the meantime, local governments plan to make use of the best available shelter.

Most of the existing public shelters are located in larger buildings and are marked with this standard yellow-and-black fallout shelter sign. Other public shelters are in smaller buildings, subways, tunnels, mines and other facilities. These also are marked with shelter signs, or would be marked in a time of emergency.

Learn the Locations of Public Shelters

An attack might come at any hour of the day or night. Therefore you should find out *now* the locations of those public fallout shelters designated by your local government for your use. If no designations have yet been made, learn the locations of public shelters that are nearest to you when you are at home, work, school, or any other place where you spend considerable time.

This advice applies to all members of the family. Your children especially should be given clear instructions *now* on where to find a fallout shelter at all times of the day, and told what other actions they should take in case an attack should occur.

A Home Shelter May Save Your Life

Public fallout shelters usually offer some advantages over home shelters. However, in many places—especially suburban and rural areas—there are few public shelters. If there is none near you, a home fallout shelter may save your life.

The basements of some homes are usable as family fallout shelters as they now stand, without any alterations or changes—especially if

24

the house has two or more stories, and its basement is below ground level.

However, most home basements would need some improvements in order to shield their occupants adequately from the radiation given off by fallout particles. Usually, householders can make these improvements themselves, with moderate effort and at low cost. Millions of homes have been surveyed for the U.S. Office of Civil Defense by the U.S. Census Bureau, and these householders have received information on how much fallout protection their basements would provide, and how to improve this protection.

Shielding Material Is Required

In setting up any home fallout shelter, the basic aim is to place enough "shielding material" between the people in the shelter and the fallout particles outside.

Shielding material is any substance that would absorb and deflect the invisible rays given off by fallout particles outside the house, and thus reduce the amount of radiation reaching the occupants of the shelter. The thicker or denser the shielding material is, the more it would protect the shelter occupants.

Some radiation protection is provided by the existing, standard walls and ceiling of a basement. But if they are not thick or dense enough, other shielding material will have to be added.

Concrete, bricks, earth and sand are some of the materials that are dense or heavy enough to provide fallout protection. For comparative purposes, 4 inches of concrete would provide the same shielding density as:

—5 to 6 inches of bricks.

—6 inches of sand or gravel___⎫ May be packed into bags, cartons, boxes,
—7 inches of earth_____⎬ or other containers for easier han-
⎭ dling.

—8 inches of hollow concrete blocks (6 inches if filled with sand).

—10 inches of water.

—14 inches of books or magazines.

—18 inches of wood.

How To Prepare a Home Shelter

If there is no public fallout shelter near your home, or if you would prefer to use a family-type shelter in a time of attack, you should prepare a home fallout shelter. Here is how to do it:

● A PERMANENT BASEMENT SHELTER. If your home basement—or one corner of it—is below ground level, your best and easiest action would be to prepare a permanent-type family shelter there. The required shielding material would cost perhaps $100–$200, and if you have basic carpentry or masonry skills you probably could do the work yourself in a short time.

Here are three methods of providing a permanent family shelter in the "best" corner of your home basement—that is, the corner which is most below ground level. If you decide to set up one of these shelters, *first get the free plan for it* by writing to Civil Defense, Army Publications Center, 2800 Eastern Blvd. (Middle River), Baltimore, Md. 21220. In ordering a plan, use the full name shown for it.

Ceiling Modification Plan A

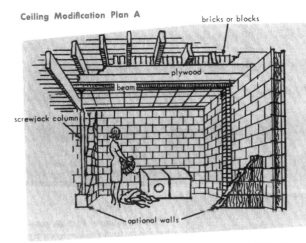

If nearly all your basement is below ground level, you can use this plan to build a fallout shelter area in one corner of it, without changing the appearance of it or interfering with its normal peacetime use.

However, if 12 inches or more of the basement wall is above ground level, this plan should *not* be used unless you add the "optional walls" shown in the sketch.

Overhead protection is obtained by screwing plywood sheets securely to the joists, and then filling the spaces between the joists with bricks or concrete blocks. An extra beam and a screwjack column may be needed to support the extra weight.

Building this shelter requires some basic woodworking skills and about $150–$200 for materials. It can be set up while the house is being built, or afterward.

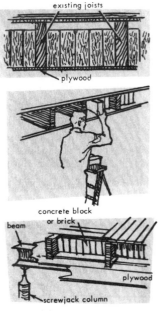

27

Alternate Ceiling Modification Plan B

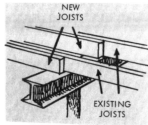

NEW JOISTS

EXISTING JOISTS

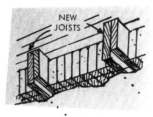

NEW JOISTS

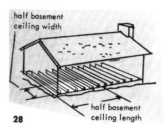

half basement ceiling width

half basement ceiling length

This is similar to Plan A, except that new extra joists are fitted into part of the basement ceiling to support the added weight of the shielding (instead of using a beam and a screwjack column).

The new wooden joists are cut to length and notched at the ends, then installed between the existing joists.

After plywood panels are screwed securely to the joists, bricks or concrete blocks are then packed tightly into the spaces between the joists. The bricks or blocks, as well as the joists themselves, will reduce the amount of fallout radiation penetrating downward into the basement.

Approximately one-quarter of the total basement ceiling should be reinforced with extra joists and shielding material.

Important: This plan (like Plan A) should *not* be used if 12 inches or more of your basement wall is above ground level, unless you add the "optional walls" inside your basement that are shown in the Plan A sketch.

Permanent Concrete Block or Brick Shelter Plan C

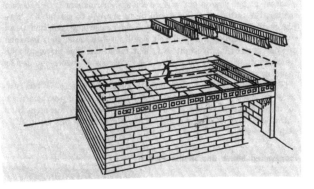

This shelter will provide excellent protection, and can be constructed easily at a cost of $150 in most parts of the country.

Made of concrete blocks or bricks, the shelter should be located in the corner of your basement that is most below ground level. It can be built low, to serve as a "sitdown" shelter; or by making it higher you can have a shelter in which people can stand erect.

The shelter ceiling, however, should *not* be higher than the outside ground level of the basement corner where the shelter is located.

The higher your basement is above ground level, the thicker you should make the walls and roof of this shelter, since your regular basement walls will provide only limited shielding against outside radiation.

Natural ventilation is provided by the shelter entrance, and by the air vents shown in the shelter wall.

This shelter can be used as a storage room or for other useful purposes in non-emergency periods.

Place entranceway on side or end not facing exposed basement wall

Increase thickness of shelter wall facing exposed basement wall by four inches

29

A PREPLANNED BASEMENT SHELTER. If your home has a basement but you do not wish to set up a permanent-type basement shelter, the next best thing would be to arrange to assemble a "preplanned" home shelter. This simply means gathering together, in advance, the shielding material you would need to make your basement (or one part of it) resistant to fallout radiation. This material could be stored in or around your home, ready for use whenever you decided to set up your basement shelter.

Here are two kinds of preplanned basement shelters. If you want to set up one of these, be sure to *get the free plan for it first* by writing to Civil Defense, Army Publications Center, 2800 Eastern Blvd. (Middle River), Baltimore, Md. 21220. Mention the full name of the plan you want.

Preplanned Snack Bar Shelter Plan D

This is a snack bar built of bricks or concrete blocks, set in mortar, in the "best" corner of your basement (the corner that is most below ground level). It can be converted quickly into a fallout shelter by lowering a strong, hinged "false ceiling" so that it rests on the snack bar.

When the false ceiling is lowered into place in a time of emergency, the hollow sections of it can be filled with bricks or concrete blocks. These can be stored conveniently nearby, or can be used as room dividers or recreation room furniture (see bench in sketch).

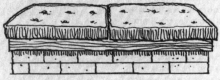

30

Preplanned Tilt-Up Storage Unit Plan E

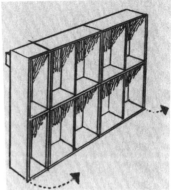

A tilt-up storage unit in the best corner of your basement is another method of setting up a "preplanned" family fallout shelter.

The top of the storage unit should be hinged to the wall. In peacetime, the unit can be used as a bookcase, pantry, or storage facility.

In a time of emergency, the storage unit can be tilted so that the bottom of it rests on a wall of bricks or concrete blocks that you have stored nearby.

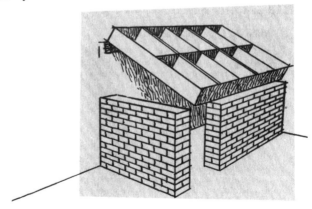

Other bricks or blocks should then be placed in the storage unit's compartments, to provide an overhead shield against fallout radiation.

The fallout protection offered by your home basement also can be increased by adding shielding material to the outside, exposed portion of your basement walls, and by covering your basement windows with shielding material.

You can cover the above-ground portion of the basement walls with earth, sand, bricks, concrete blocks, stones from your patio, or other material.

You also can use any of these substances to block basement windows and thus prevent outside fallout radiation from entering your basement in that manner.

● A PERMANENT OUTSIDE SHELTER. If your home has no basement, or if you prefer to have a permanent-type home shelter in your yard, you can obtain instructions on how to construct several different kinds of outside fallout shelters by writing to the U.S. Office of Civil Defense, Department of Defense, Washington, D.C. 20310. There is no charge for these.

When To Leave Shelter

You should not come out of shelter until you are told by authorities that it is safe to do so. Special instruments are needed to detect fallout radiation and to measure its intensity. Unless you have these instruments, you will have to depend on your local government to tell you when to leave shelter.

This information probably would be given on the radio, which is one reason why you should keep on hand a battery-powered radio that works in your shelter area.

If you came out of shelter too soon, while the fallout particles outside were still highly radioactive, you might receive enough radiation to make you sick or even kill you.

Remember that *fallout particles* can be seen, but the *rays* they give off cannot be seen. If you see unusual quantities of gritty particles outside (on window ledges, sidewalks, cars, etc.) after an attack, you should assume that they are fallout particles, and therefore stay inside your shelter until you are told it is safe to come out.

IMPROVISING FALLOUT PROTECTION

If an enemy attack should occur when you are at home, and you have made no advance shelter preparations, you still might be able to improvise a shelter either inside or outside your house. In a time of emergency, the radio broadcasts may tell you whether you have time to improvise a shelter or should take cover immediately.

An improvised shelter probably would not give you as much protection as a permanent or a preplanned family shelter, but any protection is better than none, and might save your life.

The best place to improvise a shelter would be the basement or storm cellar, if your home has one.

Shielding Material Needed

To improvise a shelter you would need shielding materials such as those mentioned on page 25—concrete blocks, bricks, sand, etc. Other things could also be used as shielding material, or to support shielding material, such as:

—House doors that have been taken off their hinges (especially heavy outside doors).

—Dressers and chests (fill the drawers with sand or earth after they are placed in position, so they won't be too heavy to carry and won't collapse while being carried).

—Trunks, boxes and cartons (fill them with sand or earth after they are placed in position).

—Tables and bookcases.

—Large appliances (such as washers and dryers).

—Books, magazines, and stacks of firewood or lumber.

—Flagstones from outside walks and patios.

Improvising a Basement Shelter

Here are two ways of improvising fallout protection in the basement of a home:

Set up a large, sturdy table or workbench in the corner of your basement that is most below ground level.

On the table, pile as much shielding material as it will hold without collapsing. Around the table, place as much shielding material as possible.

When family members are "inside the shelter"—that is, under the table—block the opening with other shielding material.

If you don't have a large table or workbench available—or if more shelter space is needed—place furniture or large appliances in the corner of the basement so they will serve as the "walls" of your shelter.

As a "ceiling" for it, use doors from the house that have been taken off their hinges. On top of the doors, pile as much shielding material as they will support. Stack other shielding material around the "walls" of your shelter.

When all persons are inside the shelter space, block the opening with shielding material.

35

Using a Storm Cellar for Fallout Protection

A below-ground storm cellar can be used as an improvised fallout shelter, but additional shielding material may be needed to provide adequate protection from fallout radiation.

If the existing roof of the storm cellar is made of wood or other light material, it should be covered with one foot of earth or an equivalent thickness of other shielding material (see page 25) for overhead shielding from fallout. More posts or braces may be needed to support the extra weight.

After the roof has been shielded, better protection can be provided by blocking the entrance way with 8-inch concrete blocks or an equivalent thickness of sandbags, bricks, earth or other shielding material, after all occupants are inside the shelter. A few inches should be left open at the top for air. After particles have stopped falling, the outside door may be left open to provide better ventilation.

If shielding material is not available for the entrance way, shelter occupants should stay as far away from it as possible. They also should raise the outside door of the storm cellar now and then to knock off any fallout particles that may have collected on it.

Using the Crawl Space Under Your House

Some homes without basements have "crawl space" between the first floor and the ground underneath the house. If you have this space under your house—and if the house is set on foundation walls, rather than on pillars—you can improvise fallout protection for your family there.

First, get access to the crawl space through the floor or through the outside foundation wall. (A trapdoor or other entry could be made now, before an emergency occurs.)

As the location for your shelter, select a crawl-space area that is under the center of the house, as far away from the outside foundation walls as possible.

36

Around the selected shelter area, place shielding material—preferably bricks or blocks, or containers filled with sand or earth—from the ground level up to the first floor of the house, so that the shielding material forms the "walls" of your shelter area. On the floor above, place other shielding material to form a "roof" for the shelter area.

If time permits, dig out more earth and make the shelter area deeper, so you can stand erect or at least sit up in it.

Improvising an Outside Shelter

If your home has no basement, no storm cellar and no protected crawl space, here are two ways of improvising fallout protection in your yard:

● Dig an L-shaped trench, about 4 feet deep and 3 feet wide. One side of the L, which will be the shelter area, should be long enough to accommodate all family members. The other side of the L can be shorter, since its purpose is to serve as an entrance-way and to reduce the amount of radiation getting into the shelter area.

Cover the entire trench with lumber (or with house doors that have been taken off their hinges), except for about 2 feet on the short side of the L, to provide access and ventilation.

On top of the lumber or doors, pile earth 1 to 2 feet high, or cover them with other shielding material.

If necessary, support or "shore up" the walls of the trench, as well as the lumber or doors, so they will not collapse.

● Dig a shallow ditch, 6 inches deep and 6 inches wide, parallel to and 4 feet from the outside wall of your house.

Remove the heaviest doors from the house. Place the bottoms of the doors in the ditch (so they won't slip), and lean the doors against the wall of the house.

On the doors, pile 12 to 18 inches of earth or sand. Stack or pile other shielding material at the sides of the doors, and also on the other side of the house wall (to protect you against radiation coming from that direction).

If possible, make the shelter area deeper by digging out more earth inside it. Also dig some other shallow ditches, to allow rain water to drain away.

37

An Improvised Shelter on the Ground Floor

If your home has no basement or storm cellar (and no crawl space that is surrounded by foundation walls up to the first floor), you can get some limited fallout protection by improvising a fallout shelter on the first or ground floor of your house. However, this type of shelter probably would not give you nearly as much protection as the other types of improvised shelters described in this chapter.

Use an inner hall, inner room or large clothes closet on the ground floor, away from outside walls and windows.

With doors, furniture and appliances, plus stacks of other shielding material, you can create an enclosure large enough to live in for a short time. If possible, use boxes filled with sand or earth as shielding material, and fill drawers and trunks with sand or earth.

If there is not room for the shielding material in the limited space of a closet or small room, you can place the material on the other sides of the walls, or on the floor overhead.

Boats as Improvised Shelters

If no better fallout protection is available, a boat with an enclosed cabin could be used. However, in addition to emergency supplies such as food, drinking water and a battery-powered radio, you should have aboard the items you would need (a broom, bucket, or pump-and-hose) to sweep off or flush off any fallout particles that might collect on the boat.

The boat should be anchored or cruised slowly at least 200 feet offshore, where the water is at least 5 feet deep. This distance from shore would protect you from radioactive fallout particles that had fallen on the nearby land. A 5-foot depth would absorb the radiation from particles falling into the water and settling on the bottom.

If particles drift down on the boat, stay inside the cabin most of the time. Go outside now and then, and sweep or flush off any particles that have collected on the boat.

38

SUPPLIES FOR FALLOUT SHELTERS

People gathered in public and private fallout shelters to escape fallout radiation after a nuclear attack would have to stay there—at least part of the time—for a week or two.

During this time they would need certain supplies and equipment in order to stay alive and well, and to cope with emergency situations that might occur in their shelters.

This chapter tells you what supplies and equipment to take with you if you go to a public fallout shelter, and what items you should keep on hand if you plan to use a family fallout shelter at home.

What To Take to a Public Fallout Shelter

To augment the supply of food and liquids usually found in large buildings, most public fallout shelters are stocked—and others are being stocked—with emergency supplies. These include water containers, emergency food rations, sanitation items, basic medical supplies, and instruments to measure the radiation given off by fallout particles.

If the public shelter you will use in a time of attack contains these or other emergency supplies, you should plan to take with you only these additional items:

—Special medicines or foods required by members of your family, such as insulin, heart tablets, dietetic food or baby food.
—A blanket for each family member.
—A battery-powered radio, a flashlight, and extra batteries.

If the public shelter you are going to does *not* contain emergency supplies, you should take with you all the above items, *plus* as much potable liquids (water, fruit and vegetable juices, etc.) and ready-to-eat food as you can carry to the shelter.

40

Stocks for a Home Shelter

If you intend to use a home fallout shelter, you should *gather together now* all the things you and your family would need for 2 weeks, even though you probably wouldn't have to remain inside shelter for that entire period.

All these items need not be stocked in your home shelter area. They can be stored elsewhere in or around your house, as long as you could find them easily and move them to your shelter area quickly in a time of emergency.

● **The Absolute Necessities.** There are a few things you *must* have. They are water, food, sanitation supplies, and any special medicines or foods needed by family members such as insulin, heart tablets, dietetic food and baby food.

● **The Complete List.** In addition to the absolute necessities, there are other important items. Some of them may be needed to save lives. At the least, they will be helpful to you. Here is a list of all major items—both essential and desirable.

WATER. This is even more important than food. Enough water should be available to give each person at least one quart per day for 14 days. Store it in plastic containers, or in bottles or cans. All should have tight stoppers. Part of your water supply might be "trapped" water in the pipes of your home plumbing system, and part of it might be in the form of bottled or canned beverages, fruit or vegetable juices, or milk. A water-purifying agent (either water-purifying tablets, or 2 percent tincture of iodine, or a liquid chlorine household bleach) should also be stored, in case you need to purify any cloudy or "suspicious" water that may contain bacteria.

FOOD. Enough food should be kept on hand to feed all shelter occupants for 14 days, including special foods needed by infants, elderly persons, and those on limited diets. Most people in shelter can get along on about half as much food as usual. If possible store canned or sealed-package foods, preferably those not requiring refrigeration or cooking. These should be replaced periodically. Here is a table showing the suggested replacement periods, in months, for some of the types of food suitable to store for emergency use.*

Milk:	Months	Cereals and baked goods:	Months
Evaporated	6	Ready-to-eat cereals:	
Nonfat dry or whole dry milk,		In metal container	12
in metal container	6	In original paper package	1
Canned meat, poultry, fish:		Uncooked cereal (quick-cook-	
Meat, poultry	18	ing or instant):	
Fish	12	In metal container	24
Mixtures of meats, vegetables,		In original paper package	12
cereal products	18	Hydrogenated (or antioxidant-	
Condensed meat-and-vegetable		treated) fats, vegetable oil	12
soups	8	Sugars, sweets, nuts:	
Fruits and vegetables:		Sugar will keep indefinitely	
Berries and sour cherries,		Hard candy, gum	18
canned	6	Nuts, canned	12
Citrus fruit juices, canned	6	Instant puddings	12
Other fruits and fruit juices,		Miscellaneous:	
canned	18	Coffee, tea, cocoa (instant)	18
Dried fruit, in metal container	6	Dry cream product (instant)	12
Tomatoes, sauerkraut, canned	6	Bouillon products	12
Other vegetables, canned (in-		Flavored beverage powders	24
cluding dry beans and dry		Salt will keep indefinitely	
peas)	18	Flavoring extracts (e.g., pep-	
		per)	24
		Soda, baking powder	12

SANITATION SUPPLIES. Since you may not be able to use your regular bathroom during a period of emergency, you should keep on hand these sanitation supplies: A metal container with a tight-fitting lid, to use as an emergency toilet; one or two large garbage cans with covers (for human wastes and garbage); plastic bags to line the toilet container; disinfectant; toilet paper; soap; wash cloths and towels; a pail or basin; and sanitary napkins.

MEDICINES AND FIRST AID SUPPLIES. This should include any medicines being regularly taken, or likely to be needed, by family members. First aid supplies should include all those found in a good first aid kit (bandages, antiseptics, etc.), plus all the items normally kept in a well-stocked home medicine chest (aspirin, thermometer, baking soda, petroleum jelly, etc.). A good first aid handbook is also recommended.

---

* This table, and other suggestions concerning emergency supplies of food and water, is contained in "Family Food Stockpile for Survival," Home and Garden Bulletin No. 77, U.S. Department of Agriculture. For sale by the Superintendent of Documents, Washington, D.C. 20402, price 10 cents.

INFANT SUPPLIES. Families with babies should keep on hand a two-week stock of infant supplies such as canned milk or baby formula, disposable diapers, bottles and nipples, rubber sheeting, blankets and baby clothing. Because water for washing might be limited, baby clothing and bedding should be stored in larger-than-normal quantities.

COOKING AND EATING UTENSILS. Emergency supplies should include pots, pans, knives, forks, spoons, plates, cups, napkins, paper towels, measuring cup, bottle opener, can opener, and pocket knife. If possible, disposable items should be stored. A heat source also might be helpful, such as an electric hot plate (for use if power is available), or a camp stove or canned-heat stove (in case power is shut off). However, if a stove is used indoors, adequate ventilation is needed.

CLOTHING. Several changes of clean clothing—especially undergarments and socks or stockings—should be ready for shelter use, in case water for washing should be scarce.

BEDDING. Blankets are the most important items of bedding that would be needed in a shelter, but occupants probably would be more comfortable if they also had available pillows, sheets, and air mattresses or sleeping bags.

FIRE FIGHTING EQUIP-MENT. Simple fire fighting tools, and knowledge of how to use them, may be very useful. A hand-pumped fire extinguisher of the inexpensive, 5-gallon, water type is preferred. Carbon tetrachloride and other vaporizing-liquid type extinguishers are not recommended for use in small enclosed spaces, because of the danger of fumes. Other useful fire equipment for home use includes buckets filled with sand, a ladder, and a garden hose.

GENERAL EQUIPMENT AND TOOLS. The essential items in this category are a battery-powered radio and a flashlight or lantern, with spare batteries. The radio might be your only link with the outside world, and you might have to depend on it for all your information and instructions, especially for advice on when to leave shelter.

Other useful items: a shovel, broom, axe, crowbar, kerosene lantern, short rubber hose for siphoning, coil of half-inch rope at least 25 feet long, coil of wire, hammer, pliers, screwdriver, wrench, nails and screws.

MISCELLANEOUS ITEMS. In addition to such practical items as matches, candles, and civil defense instructions, some personal convenience items could be brought into the home shelter if space permits. These might include books and magazines, writing materials, a clock and calendar, playing cards and hobby materials, a sewing kit, and toiletries such as toothbrushes, cosmetics, and shaving supplies.

---

*As anyone knows who is familiar with the classic *Twilight Zone* episode about a bibliophile (played by Burgess Meredith) left alone with his books after a nuclear war, another "must" is a spare set of eyeglasses.

Food Insurance, For Real

As this handbook says, during the "week or two" that people are cooped up in a fallout shelter after a nuclear attack, they will need certain food, supplies, and equipment. Of course, you already know to stock up on sanitation and medical supplies, batteries, flashlights, and water purifying tablets, and you've read about the "Grandma's Pantry" civil defense mandate popularizing freeze-dried products that could give cockroaches a run for their money in end-times endurance.

Think the shelter food and supplies industry is a thing of the past? Think again.

Julie Cazzin in the magazine *Money Sense* describes the offerings of a website called FoodInsurance.com, made famous by its celebrity spokesman, Glenn Beck: "[For $199] you get a backpack full of cooking equipment and freeze-dried meals . . . or [for $9,599] you can order enough to feed a family for a year—and still have leftovers for the four horsemen.*"

In a press release, Justen Ericksen, CEO of FoodInsurance.com, explained the company's mission: "With all of the recent natural disasters and people being forced from their homes or stuck inside without power, the time is now for people to start preparing for and becoming more educated about emergency preparedness." He continued, "You never know when a disaster or emergency might occur which makes it even more important to have a supply of food, water and other supplies that will help you survive in an emergency situation." Prepackaged meals include "lasagna, beef stroganoff and a host of other great entrees. And to top it off, this food comes packaged in a high quality backpack so you can grab it and go," according to the release.

Comedian Stephen Colbert of Comedy Central's *The Colbert Report* advertised his own satirical product in response. As reported on the food enthusiast blog *Eater*, "just in case the apocalypse comes in the form of a Food Insurance–brand beef stroganoff–transmitted virus, Colbert is offering Food Insurance Insurance for the low, low price of $89.99 a month. So you can sleep a little better at night."

---

*Of the apocalypse.

WATER, FOOD, AND SANITATION IN A SHELTER

At all times and under all conditions, human beings must have sufficient water, adequate food and proper sanitation in order to stay alive and healthy. When people are living in a fallout shelter—even for a week or two—water and food may be scarce, and it may be difficult to maintain normal sanitary conditions. Water and food supplies may have to be "managed"—that is, taken care of, kept clean, and rationed to each person in the shelter. Sanitation also may have to be managed and controlled, perhaps by setting up emergency toilets and rules to insure that they are used properly.

If you go to a *public* fallout shelter in a time of attack, you probably would not need to know a great deal about managing water, food, and sanitation. A shelter manager and his assistants would handle these problems with the cooperation of all in the shelter. He would make the best use of whatever water and food supplies were available, provide emergency toilets if necessary, set up rules for living in the shelter, arrange for the shelter occupants to carry on various activities necessary for health and well-being, and decide when it was safe for the group to leave shelter and for how long at a time.

In a *home* fallout shelter, however, you and your family would be largely on your own. You would have to take care of yourselves, solve your own problems, make your own living arrangements, subsist on the supplies you had previously stocked, and find out for yourself (probably by listening to the radio) when it was safe to leave shelter. In this situation, one of your most important tasks would be to manage your water and food supplies, and maintain sanitation. The following guidance is intended to help you do this.

Care and Use of Water Supplies

The average person in a shelter would need at least 1 quart of water or other liquids per day to drink, but more would be useful (to allow some for washing, etc.). Therefore a rationing plan might be required in your home shelter, so as to make your available liquids last for 14 days. (Many communities may continue to have potable water available, and families could relax their rationing plans.)

In addition to water stored in containers, there is usually other water available in most homes that is drinkable, such as:

—Water and other liquids normally found in the kitchen, including ice cubes, milk, soft drinks, and fruit and vegetable juices.

—Water (20 to 60 gallons) in the hot water tank.

—Water in the *flush tanks* (not the bowls) of home toilets.

—Water in the pipes of your home plumbing system. In a time of nuclear attack, local authorities may instruct householders to *turn off* the main water valves in their homes to avoid having water drain away in case of a break and loss of pressure in the water mains. With the main valve in your house closed, all the pipes in the house would still be full of water. To use this water, *turn on* the faucet that is located at the *highest* point in your house, to let air into the system; and then draw water, as needed, from the faucet that is located at the *lowest* point in your house.

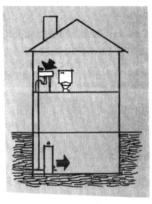

In a home shelter, occupants should drink first the water they know is uncontaminated, such as that mentioned above. Of course, if local authorities tell you the regular water is drinkable, it should be used.

If necessary, "suspicious" water—such as cloudy water from regular faucets or perhaps some muddy water from a nearby stream or pond— can be used after it has been purified. This is how to purify it:

1. Strain the water through a paper towel or several thicknesses of clean cloth, to remove dirt and fallout particles, if any. Or else let the water "settle" in a container for 24 hours, by which time any solid particles would have sunk to the bottom. A handful of clay soil in each gallon of water would help this settling process.

2. After the solid particles have been removed, boil the water if possible for 3 to 5 minutes, or add a water-purifying agent to it. This could be either: (*a*) water-purifying tablets, available at drug stores, or (*b*) two percent tincture of iodine, or (*c*) liquid chlorine household

47

bleach, provided the label says that it contains hypochlorite as its *only* active ingredient. For each gallon of water, use 4 water-purifying tablets, or 12 drops of tincture of iodine, or 8 drops of liquid chlorine bleach. If the water is cloudy, these amounts should be doubled.

There would not be much danger of drinking radioactive particles in water, as they would sink quickly to the bottom of the container or stream. Very few would dissolve in the water. Although open reservoirs might contain some radioactive iodine in the first few days after an attack, this danger is considered minor except to very young children.

Care and Use of Food Supplies

Food also should be rationed carefully in a home shelter, to make it last for at least a 2-week period of shelter occupancy. Usually, half the normal intake would be adequate, except for growing children or pregnant women.

In a shelter, it is especially important to be sanitary in the storing, handling and eating of food, so as to avoid digestive upsets or other more serious illness, and to avoid attracting vermin. Be sure to:

—Keep all food in covered containers.

—Keep cooking and eating utensils clean.

—Keep all garbage in a closed container, or dispose of it outside the home when it is safe to go outside. If possible, bury it. Avoid letting garbage or trash accumulate inside the shelter, both for fire and sanitation reasons.

Emergency Toilet Facilities

In many home shelters, people would have to use emergency toilets until it was safe to leave shelter for brief periods of time.

An emergency toilet, consisting of a watertight container with a snug-fitting cover, would be necessary. It could be a garbage container, or a pail or bucket. If the container is small, a larger container, also with a cover, should be available to empty the contents into for later disposal. If possible, both containers should be lined with plastic bags.

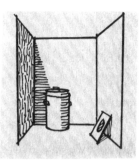

This emergency toilet could be fitted with some kind of seat, especially for children or elderly persons. Or it may be possible to remove the seat from a wooden chair, cut a hole in it, and place the container underneath. For privacy, the toilet could be screened from view.

Every time someone uses the toilet, he should pour or sprinkle into it a small amount of regular household disinfectant, such as creosol or chlorine bleach, to keep down odors and germs. After each use, the lid should be put back on.

When the toilet container needs to be emptied, and outside radiation levels permit, the contents should be buried outside in a hole 1 or 2 feet deep. This would prevent the spread of disease by rats and insects.

If the regular toilets inside the home—or the sewer lines—are not usable for any reason, an outside toilet should be built when it is safe to do so.

If anyone has been outside and fallout particles have collected on his shoes or clothing, they should be brushed off before he enters the shelter area again.

49

FIRE HAZARDS

Fire, always a danger, could be even more of a disaster during a nuclear attack emergency when the fire department might not be available to help you. Also, the risk of fire would be greater at that time.

Normal fire-prevention rules are of special importance in an emergency. They include familiar commonsense precautions such as not allowing trash to accumulate, especially near heat sources; exercising extreme caution in the use of flammable fluids such as gasoline, naphtha, etc.; storage of such fluids outdoors when possible; care in the use of electricity; repairing of faulty wiring and avoiding overloaded circuits; and repair of faulty heating systems.

These special fire precautions should be taken in a time of nuclear emergency, especially if you plan to use a home shelter:

(1) Keep some of the intense heat rays from nuclear explosions from entering your house by closing your doors, windows, venetian blinds, window shades and drapes. If the climate will not permit this for an extended period of time, close as many as possible, then close the rest when the Attack Warning Signal is given.

(2) Unless local authorities advise otherwise, fill buckets, bathtubs and other containers with water, for use in emergency fire fighting.

If a fire does occur, your home might be saved if you know how to fight fires, and have on hand some basic firefighting tools. These should include a garden hose, a ladder, buckets filled with sand, containers filled with water, and a fire extinguisher. Keep in mind that vaporizing-liquid types of fire extinguishers can produce dangerous fumes when used in small enclosed spaces.

Remember the 3 basic ways to put out a fire:

⬤ Take away its fuel.

⬤ Take away its air (smother it).

⬤ Cool it with water or fire-extinguisher chemicals.

Ordinary fires should be fought by:

—Getting the burning material out of the house (carry it out, or throw it out of a door or window if you can); or
—Putting out the fire with water, sand, earth or fire-extinguisher chemicals; or
—Smothering the fire with a rug or blanket, preferably wet.

53

Special types of fires require special methods:

—If it is an *electrical fire*, be sure to shut off the electricity first. Then put out the flames with water or anything else available. If you can't shut off the electricity, don't use water on an electrical fire.

—If it is an *oil or grease fire*, shut off the supply of whatever is burning. Then smother the flames with sand, earth, rugs, or other heavy materials. Don't use water.

—If it is a *gas fire*, shut off the gas supply. Then use water, sand, or earth to put out whatever is burning.

III.
MAD as Hell
1970s

MAD was a horrifying and nihilistic concept, so people tried to find ways to circumvent its logic. Both the Americans and Soviets worked on developing anti-ballistic missiles to shoot down incoming warheads. They found this a tough technical problem to solve, yet worried that one side or the other might suddenly gain the ability and thus be able to protect itself from retaliation after destroying the enemy with a first strike of nuclear weapons. Having the logic of MAD subverted was even more frightening than the doctrine itself. The Anti-Ballistic Missile (ABM) Treaty was signed in 1972 to stop the development and deployment of such weapons.

When would MAD apply and when would it not? In a possible future war, if a Soviet submarine were to destroy an entire American naval task force with a single nuclear torpedo, would America respond with nuclear torpedoes of its own or escalate to strategic weapons? If Soviet armies were overrunning West Germany, aided by the selective use of tactical nuclear weapons to destroy concentrations of NATO troops, would the Americans and their allies respond with tactical nuclear weapons or escalate immediately to strategic weapons?

The Carter Administration developed a "countervailing strategy" in the late 1970s, an attempt to add some possibility for diplomacy during a nuclear war. Administration officials also tried to make the idea of nuclear war a bit more palatable by publicly targeting strategic nuclear weapon missile launch, national leadership sites, military sites, and industrial sites. While the cities themselves were no longer targeted in an attempt to destroy population, the allowed sites were often in or near major cities.

Meanwhile, three other nations joined the nuclear club. The United Kingdom exploded its first atomic bomb at sea off of northwestern

Australia in 1952. British scientists had worked on the Manhattan Project, and with American help, building the country's own nuclear weapons was only a matter of time. The French exploded their first atomic bomb in 1960 in the deep desert of Algeria. Both the United Kingdom and France wanted independent nuclear forces so that they would not be too tightly bound to their American ally. France also developed its own bombers and missiles, and moved testing to Polynesia after Algeria was no longer available. China had been working with the Soviets to develop its own atomic bomb, but after a falling out between the two communist giants, the Chinese pushed forward on their own and exploded their first atomic bomb at Lop Nur in 1964.

France, Britain, and China opted to build smaller forces, enough to provide a substantial sting if it came to nuclear war but not the massive overkill of the Americans and Soviets. The American nuclear stockpile peaked in 1967 at 31,255 warheads.. The Soviet stockpile probably topped 40,000 in the mid-1980s. The American nuclear stockpile in 2009 had dropped to 5,113 warheads, a decline matched by a similar decline in the Soviet stockpile, a more manageable number of weapons that are easier to keep counted and protected, though still enough to destroy the world. The common thriller plot of stealing a nuclear weapon is not farfetched, though both the United States and the Soviet Union developed technologies to limit the ability of those weapons to be used without the proper electronic codes. Safety technologies were also developed in order to limit the possibility of an accidental explosion.

These five nations (U.S., U.S.S.R., U.K., France, and China) were considered the original "nuclear club." Concerned about the hazards that might emerge if even more nations gained nuclear weapons, these original nations made a serious effort either to talk other nations out of acquiring nuclear weapons of their own or to prevent the spread of technology and fissionable material necessary to build nuclear weapons. The Nuclear Non-Proliferation Treaty (NPT) of 1968 recognized that five nuclear weapon states already existed and prohibited other nations from acquiring nuclear weapons. The International Atomic Energy Agency (IAEA), an independent organization founded in 1957 that is sponsored by the United Nations, implemented a system of inspections to prevent the proliferation of nuclear weapons. India, Pakistan, and Israel have refused to sign the NPT. Technologically advanced nations, such as Japan, Taiwan, Canada, and West Germany, have chosen to sign the NPT and have not developed nuclear weapons, though they could probably do so within the space of a year if they chose to.

The governments of the United States and Soviet Union recognized that the arms race in nuclear weapons was expensive and that perhaps they had enough weapons and delivery systems already. In a period of diplomatic détente in the 1970s, the two superpowers negotiated the Strategic Arms Limitation Treaty (SALT I) while also negotiating the ABM Treaty. The numbers of land-launched and submarine-launched missiles were frozen at current levels, but technology had already been developed to make these limitations less useful. To increase the possible effect from a single delivery vehicle, the MIRV (multiple independently targetable reentry vehicle) was developed in the 1960s. After launch and the boost phase, the warhead payload of an ICBM had enough velocity to fly across the polar regions between the Soviet Union and Canada and curl down on its target. The payload package could launch up to ten separate MIRV warheads, giving each missile much more potential punch.

The SALT II agreement was negotiated by the Carter Administration and signed in 1979, banning the development of new land-based ballistic missiles and limiting MIRV systems. The treaty was never ratified by the U.S. Senate, though the Reagan Administration honored it until opting out of it in 1986, after accusing the Soviets of having violated the treaty. As the Soviet Union collapsed, a Strategic Arms Reduction Treaty (START I) was negotiated that actually reduced the number of nuclear weapons. Signed in 1991, and coming into force in 1994, the treaty was honored by Russia, the successor state to the Soviet Union. In addition to substantially reducing the number of nuclear delivery vehicles over a seven-year period, the treaty implemented strict verification processes. Verification was something that the Americans had always wanted but the Soviets had always resisted, not liking the idea of American military officers being able to legally demand the right to search suspicious facilities in their country. START II was signed in 1993, which banned MIRV weapons on ICBMs. Later efforts have continued to decrease the number of nuclear delivery vehicles in both Russia and the United States, though both nations still have much larger nuclear weapons forces than any other nation.

In the 1980s, the Reagan Administration started intensive research into the idea of a Strategic Defense Initiative (SDI), which would protect the United States from Soviet missiles with a collection of both satellite-based and ground-based lasers, particle beams, and small rocket interceptors. This became colloquially known as "Star Wars" and, in terms of its grandiose ambitions, was an abject failure. Edward Teller, father of the hydrogen bomb, strongly supported Reagan in his plans, though it was unclear how he expected the technical challenges to be overcome. The original ambition of a near-perfect shield formed by orbiting satellites armed with anti-missile missiles and beam weapons quickly became more limited in concept once it became apparent that the Soviet Union could build more intercontinental ballistic missiles much faster and cheaper than any possible SDI system that could be deployed. While research continued on a much reduced scale, SDI disappeared as a strategic vision until the second Bush Administration revived it in 2001.

India joined the nuclear club in 1974 with an underground nuclear test. This alarmed Pakistan, which ardently strived to catch up with its larger neighbor. China provided extensive technological support to Pakistan in its effort. In 1998, Pakistan announced its success by testing a nuclear weapon underground. India reacted by testing three of its own weapons simultaneously. Pakistan responded to this provocation by announcing that it had just tested five weapons simultaneously (though an argument can be made that the test really only involved two weapons).

The chief Pakistani nuclear scientist, A. Q. Khan, believed that all nations should have their own weapons and sold nuclear knowledge and technology to both Libya and North Korea. Libya later abandoned its program, but the North Koreans worked diligently on the problem and announced that they had exploded a small atomic bomb underground in 2006. External monitoring by the United States and other nations led to the conclusion that the fission-based device had actually fizzled and had a very low yield. North Korea tried again three years later and had a more successful underground test.

Two other nations have developed nuclear weapons but have not tested them. With substantial French help, Israel developed a nuclear weapons project in the 1950s and 1960s. France eventually withdrew its cooperation, but the Israelis pushed forward to build an arsenal that is estimated at 150–200 weapons. Israeli nuclear weapons are shrouded in secrecy, a curious arrangement where the Israeli government still denies that it has such weapons, yet other nations know that Israel has them, and the required missiles or aircraft to delivery them. The Israelis never announced their admission to the nuclear club with a test, showing that they have enough confidence in their designs to believe that they will work. It is thought by some that a mysterious pair of blips detected by an American Vela spy satellite in 1979 off the coast of South Africa was an open-water test.

South Africa, with Israeli help, developed its own nuclear weapons. Eventually up to seven bombs were built, but by 1990, as apartheid was ending, the South African government chose to end the entire program and dismantle the bombs. The South Africans also never announced their membership in the nuclear club with an open test, though they may have done so with the Vela incident. It should be pointed out that the Americans and Soviets have developed such sophisticated sensors, placed around the world and in space (including the Vela satellites), that setting off a nuclear weapon and not being caught is essentially impossible.

While the Soviets had proven to be rational actors who adhered to MAD, an irrational nation could just do something crazy and hit America with a nuclear weapon. In 2002, the Bush Administration withdrew from the ABM Treaty, wanting to deploy a limited ABM system in Alaska to counter a possible missile from a rogue nation, such as North Korea. There was no intent, or ability, to create a system that could stop a Soviet strike, which would employ so many more missiles.

People were becoming less willing to accept civil defense reassurances in the face of MAD, especially after Watergate turned a generation of Americans into cynics. What follows is the cold, hard scientific truth about what the experience of a Soviet attack would be like, excerpted from *The Effects of Nuclear War* (1979). It was not a pretty thing to ponder, but most Americans weren't in a mood to accept the optimistic messages of past government brochures in the wake of Richard Nixon, oil shortages, and a recession that would linger into the early 1980s.

Surviving the Unsurvivable

In *Emergency: This Book Will Save Your Life*, author Neil Strauss recalls talking with his father about life during the Cold War, when "school assemblies . . . showed films about what to do in case of a nuclear attack" and "Russia had missiles pointed at [Strauss's] home city." He asked his father if he had been scared for their family:

> "Not really," he replied. "I'd say that right now [post-9/11] is the scariest time I've been alive."
>
> Considering that my father had lived through World War II and the Cold War, in addition to serving as an army lieutenant in Korea, his answer gave some legitimacy to my concerns. "Why is it scarier now?" I asked him.
>
> "In the Cold War, because of mutually assured destruction, you didn't think about the Russians sending their nuclear things over. But now, with terrorists, you don't know what's going to happen. They've killed innocent people everywhere on the planet. So it's scary at home and it's scary when you travel. Nothing's safe anymore."

Later, Strauss's father gave him Life After Doomsday by Bruce Clayton. Strauss called it "a bible for the burgeoning survivalist movement." In June 1983, Gaddis Smith reviewed *Life After Doomsday* and some similar books for the Bulletin of the Atomic Scientists: "There are several ways to respond to these manuals and their message. Ridicule is easy." The review calls Clayton "fervent in his denunciations" of "exaggerated and unscientific" depictions of "horrendous consequences of nuclear war" by "disarmament activists." Smith explained that Clayton and other survivalist authors rejected the "paralyzing despair" of believing nuclear war is not survivable.

But Smith wonders, "Is the behavior advocated by these books [by Clayton and others] dangerous?" Her answer: "Yes. It is behavior bereft of any sense of the meaning of life. There are no values. No reality, except that of shooting those who would invade your shelter. . . . [T]he only indisputable scientific fact is that no one will die from nuclear war if there is no nuclear war."

A SOVIET
ATTACK SCENARIO

From

THE EFFECTS OF NUCLEAR WAR

CONGRESS OF THE UNITED STATES

Office of Technology Assessment
Washington, D.C. 20510

1979

A SOVIET ATTACK ON U.S. MILITARY
AND ECONOMIC TARGETS

This case discusses a massive attack that one normally associates with all-out nuclear war. The attack uses thousands of warheads to attack urban-industrial targets, strategic targets, and other military targets. The number of deaths and the damage and destruction inflicted on the U.S. society and economy by the sheer magnitude of such an attack would place in question whether the United States would ever recover its position as an organized, industrial, and powerful country.

OTA favored examining purely retaliatory strikes for both sides, but all of the available executive branch studies involved Soviet preemption and U.S. retaliation. However, the differences between a Soviet first strike and a retaliation do not appear to be appreciably large in terms of damage to the civilian structure. Like the United States, the Soviets have a secure second-strike force in their SLBMs and are assumed to target them generally against the softer urban-industrial targets. Moreover, a U.S. first strike would be unlikely to destroy the bulk of Soviet ICBMs before they could be launched in retaliation.

The effects of a large Soviet attack against the United States would be devastating. The most immediate effects would be the loss of millions of human lives, accompanied by similar incomprehensible levels of injuries, and the physical destruction of a high percentage of U.S. economic and industrial capacity. The full range of effects resulting from several thousand warheads—most having yields of a megaton or greater—impacting on or near U.S. cities can only be discussed in terms of uncertainty and speculation. The executive branch studies that addressed this level of attack report a wide range of fatality levels reflecting various assumptions about the size of the attack, the protective posture of the population, and the proportion of air bursts to ground burst weapons.

The DOD 1977 study estimated that 155 million to 165 million Americans would be killed by this attack if no civil defense measures were taken and all weapons were ground burst. DCPA looked at a similar attack in 1978 where only half the weapons were ground burst; it reduced the fatality estimate to 122 million. ACDA's analysis of a similar case estimated that 105 million to 131 million would die.

If people made use of existing shelters near their homes, the 155 million to 165 million fatality estimate would be reduced to 110 million to 145 million, and the 122 million fatalities to 100 million. The comparable ACDA fatality estimate drops to 76 million to 85 million. Again ACDA gets a lower figure through assuming air bursts for about 60 percent of the incoming weapons. Finally, if urban populations were evacuated from risk areas, the estimated prompt fatality levels would be substantially reduced. The DOD study showed fatalities of 40 million to 55 million, with DCPA showing a very large drop to 20 million from the 100 million level. The primary reason for the 2-to-1 differential is the degree of protection from fallout assumed for the evacuated population.

In summary, U.S. fatality estimates range from a high of 155 million to 165 million to a low of 20 million to 55 million. Fatalities of this magnitude beg the question of injuries to the survivors. None of the analyses attempted to estimate injuries with the same precision used in estimated fatalities. However, DCPA did provide injury estimates ranging from 33 million to 12 million, depending on circumstances. An additional point worth noting is that all of the fatality figures just discussed are for the first 30 days following the attack; they do not account for subsequent deaths among the injured or from economic disruption and deprivation.

THE FIRST FEW HOURS

The same devastation caused by a single l-Mt weapon would take place in 30 or so other major cities (with populations of a million or greater), including the Detroit metropolitan area. A l-Mt explosion on the surface leaves a crater about 1,000 feet [300 m] in diameter and 200 feet [61 m] deep, surrounded by a rim of highly radioactive soil about twice this diameter thrown out of the crater. Out to a distance of 0.6 miles [1 km] from the center there will be nothing recognizable remaining, with the exception of some massive concrete bridge abutments and building foundations. At 0.6 miles some heavily damaged highway bridge sections will remain, but little else until 1.3 miles [2.1 km], where a few very strongly constructed buildings with poured reinforced concrete walls will survive, but with the interiors totally destroyed by blast entering the window openings. A distance of 1.7 miles [2.7 km] is the closest range where any significant structure will remain standing.

Of the 70,000 people in this area during nonworking hours, there will be virtually no survivors. (See table 1.) Fatalities during working hours in this business district would undoubtedly be much higher. The estimated daytime population of the "downtown" area is something over 200,000 in contrast to the census data of about 15,000. If the attack occurred during this time, the fatalities would be increased by 130,000 and injuries by 45,000 over the estimates in table 1. Obviously there would be some reduction in casualties in outlying residential areas where the daytime population would be lower.

Between 1.7 and the 2.7 miles from the blast, typical commercial and residential multistory buildings will have the walls completely blown out, but increasingly at the greater distances the skeletal structure will remain standing.

Individual residences in this region will be totally destroyed, with only foundations and basements remaining, and the debris quite uniformly distributed over the area. Heavy industrial plants will be destroyed in the inner part of the ring, but some industry will remain functional towards the outer edge. The debris depth that will clutter the streets will naturally depend on both the building heights and how close together they are spaced. Typical depths might range from tens of feet in the downtown area where buildings are 10 to 20 stories high, down to several inches where buildings are lower and streets broader in the sector to the west and north, In this band, blast damage alone will destroy all automobiles, while some heavier commercial vehicles (firetrucks and repair vehicles) will survive near the outer edges. However, few vehicles will have been sufficiently protected from debris to remain useful. The parking lots of both Cobb Field and Tiger Stadium will contain nothing driveable.

Table 1.—Casualty Estimates (in thousands)

Region (mi)	Area (mi²)	Population	Fatalities	Injuries	Uninjured
0–1.7	9.1	70	70	0	0
1.7–2.7	13.8	250	130	100	20
2.7–4.7	46.5	400	20	180	200
4.7–7.4	102.6	600	0	150	450

In this same ring, which contains a nighttime population of about 250,000, about half will be fatalities, with most of the remainder being injured. Most deaths will occur from collapsing buildings. Although many fires will be started, only a small percentage of the buildings are likely to continue to burn after the blast wave passes. The mechanics of fire spread in a heavily damaged and debris strewn area are not well understood. However, it is probable that fire spread would be slow and there would be no firestorm. For unprotected people, the initial nuclear radiation would be lethal out to 1.7 miles [2.7 km], but be insignificant in its prompt effects (50 rems) at 2.0 miles [3.2 km]. Since few people inside a 2-mile ring will survive the blast, and they are very likely to be in strong buildings that typically have a 2 to 5 protection factor, the additional fatalities and injuries from initial radiation should be small compared to other uncertainties.

The number of casualties from thermal burns depends on the time of day, season, and atmospheric visibility. Modest variations in these factors produce huge changes in vulnerability to burns. For example, on a winter night less than 1 percent of the population might be exposed to direct thermal radiation, while on a clear summer weekend afternoon more than 25 percent might be exposed (that is, have no structure between the fireball and the person). When visibility is 10 miles [16 km], a 1-Mt explosion produces second-degree burns at a distance of 6 miles [10 km], while under circumstances when visibility is 2 miles [3 km], the range of second-degree burns is only 2.7 miles [4.3 km]. Table 2 shows how this variation could cause deaths from thermal radiation to vary between 1,000 and 190,000, and injuries to vary between 500 and 75,000.

In the band from 2.7 to 4.7 miles [4.4 to 7.6 km], large buildings will have lost windows and frames, interior partitions, and, for those with light-walled construction, most of the contents of upper floors will have been blown out into the streets. Load-bearing wall buildings at the University of Detroit will be severely cracked. Low residential buildings will be totally destroyed or severely damaged. Casualties are estimated to be about 50 percent in this region, with the majority of these injured. There will still be substantial debris in the streets, but a very significant number of cars and trucks will remain operable. In this zone, damage to heavy industrial plants, such as the Cadillac plant, will be severe, and most planes and hangars at the Detroit City Airport will be destroyed.

In this ring only 5 percent of the population of about 400,000 will be killed, but nearly half will be injured (table 1). This is the region of the most severe fire hazard, since fire ignition and spread is more likely in partly damaged buildings than in completely flattened areas. Perhaps 5 percent of the buildings would be initially ignited, with fire spread to adjoining buildings highly likely if their separation is less than 50 feet [15 m]. Fires will continue to spread for 24 hours at least, ultimately destroying about half the buildings. However, these estimates are extremely uncertain, as they are based on poor data and unknown weather conditions. They are also made on the assumption that no effective effort is made by the uninjured half of the population in this region to prevent the ignition or spread of fires.

As table 2 shows, there would be between 4,000 and 95,000 additional deaths from thermal radiation in this band, assuming a visibility of 10 miles [16 km]. A 2-mile [3 km] visibility would produce instead between 1,000 and 11,000 severe injuries, and many of these would subsequently die because adequate medical treatment would not be available.

In the outermost band (4.7 to 7.4 miles [7.6 to 11.9 km]) there will be only light damage to commercial structures and moderate damage to residences. Casualties are estimated at 25 percent injured and only an insignificant number killed (table 1). Under the range of conditions displayed in table 2, there will be an additional 3,000 to 75,000 burn injuries requiring specialized medical care. Fire ignitions should be comparatively rare (limited to such kindling material as newspaper and dry leaves) and easily controlled by the survivors.

Whether fallout comes from the stem or the cap of the mushroom is a major concern in the general vicinity of the detonation because of the time element and its effect on general emergency operations. Fallout from the stem starts building after about 10 minutes, so during the first hour after detonation it represents the prime radiation threat to emergency crews. The affected area would have a radius of about 6.5 miles [10.5 km] with a hot-spot a distance downwind that depends on the wind velocity. If a 15-mph wind from the southwest is assumed, an elliptical area of about 1 mi^2 [260 hectares] would cause an average exposure of 300 rems in the first hour to people with no fallout protection at all. A larger ellipse around that would receive 150 rems in the first hour. But the important feature of short-term (up to 1 hour) fallout is the relatively small area covered by life-threatening radiation levels compared to the area covered by blast damage.

Table 2.—Burn Casualty Estimates (1 Mt on Detroit)

Distance from blast (mi)	Survivors of blast effects	Fatalities (eventual)		Injuries	
		2-mile visibility	10-mile visibility	2-mile visibility	10-mile visibility
(1 percent of population exposed to line of sight from fireball)					
0–1.7	0	0	0	0	0
1.7–2.7	120,000	1,200	1,200	0	0
2.7–4.7	380,000	0	3,800	500	0
4.7–7.4	600,000	0	2,600	0	3,000
Total (rounded) ..		1,000	8,000	500	3,000
(25 percent of population exposed to line of sight from fireball)					
0–1.7	0	0	0	0	0
1.7–2.7	120,000	30,000	30,000	0	0
2.7–4.7	380,000	0	95,000	11,000	0
4.7–7.4	600,000	0	66,000	0	75,000
Total (rounded) ..		30,000	190,000	11,000	75,000

These calculations arbitrarily assume that exposure to more than 6.7 cal/cm^2 produces eventual death, and exposure to more than 3.4 cal/cm^2 produces a significant injury, requiring specialized medical treatment.

Starting in about an hour, the main fallout from the cloud itself will start to arrive, with some of it adding to the already-deposited local stem fallout, but the bulk being distributed in an elongated downwind ellipse.

As a complement to the preceding description of physical destruction, the status of the various infrastructure elements of the Detroit metropolitan area, and the potential for their recovery, can be addressed. The reader should understand that this tutorial considers Detroit to be the only damaged area in the United States, that there is no other threat that would prevent survivors and those in surrounding areas from giving all possible aid, and that Federal and State governments will actively organize outside assistance.

The near half-million injured present a medical task of incredible magnitude. Hospitals and beds within 4 miles of the blast would be totally destroyed. Another 15 percent in the 4- to 8-mile distance range will be severely damaged, leaving 5,000 beds remaining outside the region of significant damage. Since this is only 1 percent of the number of injured, these beds are incapable of providing significant medical assistance. In the first few days, transport of injured out of the damaged area will be severely hampered by debris clogging the streets. In general, only the nonprofessional assistance of nearby survivors can hope to hold down the large number of subsequent deaths that would otherwise occur. Even as transportation for the injured out of the area becomes available in subsequent days, the total medical facilities of the United States will be severely overburdened, since in 1977 there were only 1,407,000 hospital beds in the whole United States. Burn victims will number in the tens of thousands; yet in 1977 there were only 85 specialized burn centers, with probably 1,000 to 2,000 beds, in the entire United States.

The total loss of all utilities in areas where there has been significant physical damage to the basic structure of buildings is inevitable. The electric power grid will show both the inherent strength and weakness of its complex network. The collapse of buildings and the toppling of trees and utility poles, along with the injection of tens of thousands of volts of EMP into wires, will cause the immediate loss of power in a major sector of the total U.S. power grid.

The water distribution system will remain mostly intact. The gas distribution system will receive loss of pressure from numerous broken service connections, some broken mains, and numerous resulting fires. Service will be slowly restored only as utility repairmen and service equipment are brought in from surrounding areas.

Rescue and recovery operations will depend heavily on the reestablishment of transportation, which in Detroit relies on private cars, buses, and commercial trucks, using a radial interstate system and a conventional urban grid. Since bridges and overpasses are surprisingly immune to blast effects, those interstate highways and broad urban streets without significant structures nearby will survive as close as 3 miles from the blast and can be quickly restored to use on clearing away minor amounts of debris. However, the majority of urban streets will be cluttered with varying quantities of debris.

The Detroit city airport will have essentially all of its aircraft and facilities destroyed. Usually runways can be quickly restored to use following minor debris removal but, in this particular example with the southwest wind, the airport is the center of the fallout hot spot from the dust column as well as of the intensive fallout from the cloud. Thus, cleanup efforts to restore flight operations could not commence for 2 weeks at the earliest, with the workers involved in the cleanup receiving 100 rems accumulated during the third week. The Detroit Metropolitan Wayne County Airport and the Willow Run Airport are far outside the blast effects area and would be available as soon as the regional power grid electric service was restored.

The main train station, near the Detroit-Windsor highway tunnel, would have suffered major damage, but since few people commute to the downtown area by train, its loss would not be a major factor in the overall paralysis of transportation. The surrounding industry depends heavily on rail transportation, but rail equipment and lines will usually survive wherever the facilities they support survive.

Most gasoline fuel oil tanks are located out beyond Dearborn and Lincoln Park and, at 16 miles from the detonation, will have suffered no damage. Arrival of fuel should not be impeded, but its distribution will be totally dependent on cleanup of streets and highways.

The civil defense control center, located just beyond the Highland Park area, should be able to function without impairment. Commercial communications systems (television and base radio transmitters) will be inoperable both from the loss of commercial power in the area and, for those facilities in the blast area, from EMP. Those not blast damaged should be restored in several days. In the meantime, mobile radio systems will provide the primary means of communicating into the heavily damaged areas. The telephone system will probably remain largely functional in those areas where the lines have survived structural damage in collapsing buildings, or street damage in areas where they are not buried.

Many cities with smaller populations than Detroit would be similarly destroyed. The effects on U.S. society would be catastrophic.

The majority of urban deaths will be blast induced, e.g., victims of collapsing buildings, flying debris, being blown into objects, etc. Except for administering to the injured, the next most pressing thing (probably ahead of handling the dead) for most survivors would be to get reliable information about what has occurred, what is taking place, and what is expected. Experience has shown that in a disaster situation, timely and relevant information is critical to avoiding panic, helpful in organizing and directing productive recovery efforts, and therapeutic to the overall psychological and physical well being of those involved. Presumably, the civil preparedness functions would be operating well enough to meet some of this need.

Rescuing and treating the injured will have to be done against near insurmountable odds. Fire and rescue vehicles and equipment not destroyed will find it impossible to move about in any direction. Fires will be raging, water mains will be flooding, powerlines will be down, bridges will be gone, freeway overpasses will be collapsed, and debris will be everywhere. People will be buried under heavy debris and structures, and without proper equipment capable of lifting such loads, the injured cannot be reached and will not survive. The fortunate ones that rescuers can reach will then be faced with the unavailability of treatment facilities. Hospitals and clinics in downtown areas would likely have been destroyed along with most of their stocks of medical supplies. Doctors, nurses, and technicians needed to man makeshift treatment centers are likely to have been among the casualties. The entire area of holocaust will be further numbed by either the real or imagined danger of fallout. People will not know whether they should try to evacuate their damaged city, or attempt to seek shelter from fallout in local areas and hope there will be no new attacks. No doubt some of both would be done.

If this situation were an isolated incident or even part of a small number of destroyed cities in an otherwise healthy United States, outside help would certainly be available. But if 250 U.S. cities are struck and damaged to similar levels, then one must ask, "Who is able to help?" Smaller towns are limited in the amount of assistance they can provide their metropolitan neighbors. It is doubtful that there would be a strong urge to buck the tide of evacuation in order to reach a place where most of the natives are trying to leave. Additionally, the smaller cities and towns would have their own preparedness problems of coping with the anticipated arrival of fallout plus the influx of refugees. In light of these and other considerations, it appears that in an attack of this magnitude, there is likely not to be substantial outside assistance for the targeted areas until prospective helpers are convinced of two things: the attack is over, and fallout intensity has reached safe levels. Neither of these conditions is likely to be met in the first few hours.

Patton Weighs In

The following paper by a future four-star general contains a certain prescience about the coming weaponry in the decades to follow.

The Effect of Weapons on War
Major George S. Patton, Jr., Cavalry
Cavalry Journal
November 1930

When Samson took the fresh jawbone of an ass and slew a thousand men therewith, he probably started such a vogue for the weapon, particularly among the Philistines, that for years no prudent donkey dared to bray. Yet, despite its initial popularity it was discarded and now appears only as a barrage instrument in acrimonious debate.

Turning from sacred to profane history, we find it replete with similar instances of military instruments, each in its day heralded as the "*dernier cri*," the key to victory. Yet, each in its turn retiring to its proper place of useful, though not spectacular, importance.

Of yore, the chariot, the elephant, armor of various sorts, Greek fire, the longbow, and gunpowder, to mention only a few, were each acclaimed. Within our memory the dynamite gun and the submarine were similarly lauded. Today, the tank, gas, and the airplane are aspirants for a place on the list.

In investigating the question, let us begin by picturing, if we may, the cataclysmic effect produced on primordial society by the first savage who chanced to use a splintered rib as a means of giving point to his demands for a larger share of meat and women. How they gibbered around the half-gnawed bison as with signs and gutturals they described the fight. How their hairy bellies palpitated as into the twilight of their minds the idea flickered that they, too, might be so struck. "Romance is dead," they growled, "The day of tooth and fingernail is done."

THE FIRST FEW DAYS

Survivors will continue to be faced with the decision whether to evacuate or seek shelter in place during this interval. The competence and credibility of authority will be under continuous question. Will survivors be told the facts, or what is best for them to know, and who decides? Deaths will have climbed due to untreated injuries, sickness, shock, and poor judgment. Many people will decide to attempt evacuation simply to escape the reality of the environment. For those staying, it likely means the beginning of an extended period of shelter survival. Ideally, shelters must protect from radiation while meeting the minimums of comfort, subsistence, and personal hygiene. Convincing people to remain in shelters until radiation levels are safely low will be difficult, but probably no more so than convincing them that it is safe to leave on the basis of a radiation-rate meter reading. There will be unanswerable questions on long-term effects.

Sheltering the survivors in the populous Boston to Norfolk corridor will present unprecedented problems. Almost one-fifth of the U.S. population lives in this small, 150- by 550-mile [250 by 900 km] area. Aside from the threat of destruction from direct attack, these populations are in the path of fallout from attacks on missile silos and many industrial targets in the Pittsburgh, St. Louis, and Duluth triangle. Depending on the winds at altitude, the fallout from the Midwest will begin arriving 12 to 30 hours after the attack.

At the time when fallout radiation first becomes intense, only a fraction of the surviving urban population will be in adequate fallout shelters. Those that are sheltered will face a variety of problems: making do with existing stocks of food, water, and other necessities or else minimizing exposure while leaving the shelter for supplies; dealing with problems of sanitation, which will not only create health hazards but also exacerbate the social tensions of crowds of frightened people in a small space; dealing with additional people wanting to enter the shelter, who would not only want to share scarce supplies but might bring contamination in with them; dealing with disease, which would be exacerbated not only by the effects of radiation but by psychosomatic factors; and finally judging when it is safe to venture out. Boredom will gradually replace panic, but will be no easier to cope with. Those with inadequate shelters or no shelters at all will die in large numbers, either from lethal doses of radiation or from the combination of other hazards with weakness induced by radiation sickness.

The conditions cited above are generally more applicable to urbanites who are trying to survive. The problems of rural survivors are somewhat different, some being simpler—others more complex. With warning, people living in rural areas could readily fabricate adequate fallout shelters. However, it might be more difficult for a rural shelteree to have current and accurate information regarding fallout intensity and location. The farm family is likely not to have suffered the traumatic exposure to death and destruction, and consequently is probably better prepared psychologically to spend the required time in a shelter. (Possible consequences to livestock and crops are addressed later in this section.)

Outdoor activity in or near major cities that were struck would likely be limited to emergency crews attempting to control fires or continuing to rescue the injured. Crews would wear protective clothing but it would be necessary to severely limit the total work hours of any one crew member, so as not to risk dangerous accumulations of radiation. Areas not threatened by fallout could begin more deliberate fire control and rescue operations. Whether a national facility would survive to identify weapons impact points and predict fallout patterns is doubtful.

The extent of death and destruction to the Nation would still be unknown. For the most part, the agencies responsible for assembling such information would not be functioning. This task would have to wait until the numbing effect of the attack had worn off, and the Government could once again begin to function, however precariously.

THE SHELTER PERIOD (UP TO A MONTH)

As noted earlier, after the initial shock period, including locating and getting settled in shelters, the problem of sheltering large masses of people will be compounded as the shelter time extends. Survival will remain the key concern. People will experience or witness radiation death and sickness for the first time. Many previously untreated injuries will require medical attention, if permanent damage or death to the individual is to be avoided. Stockpiles of medical, food, and water supplies are sure to become items of utmost concern. Whether some people can safely venture outside the shelter for short periods to forage for uncontaminated supplies will depend on fallout intensity, and the availability of reliable means of measuring it.

This period will continue to be marked by more inactivity than activity. Many areas will have been freed from the fallout threat either by rain, shifting winds, or distance from the detonations. But economic activity will not resume immediately. Workers will remain concerned about their immediate families and may not want to risk leaving them. Information and instruction may not be forthcoming, and if it is, it may be confusing and misleading, and of little use. Uncertainty and frustration will plague the survivors, and even the most minor tasks will require efforts far out of proportion to their difficulty. Many will interpret this as symptomatic of radiation effects and become further confused and depressed. The overall psychological effects will likely worsen until they become a major national concern, perhaps on the same level with other incapacitating injuries.

Deaths occurring within the first 30 days of an attack are categorized as prompt fatalities. This duration is a computation standard more than it is related to specific death-producing effects, and is the basis for most fatality estimates. However, deaths from burns, injuries, and radiation sickness can be expected to continue far beyond this particular interval.

THE RECUPERATION PERIOD

Whether economic recovery would take place, and if so what form it would take, would depend both on the physical survival of enough people and resources to sustain recovery, and on the question of whether these survivors could adequately organize themselves.

Physical survival of some people is quite probable, and even a population of a few million can sustain a reasonably modern economy under favorable circumstances. The survivors would not be a cross-section of prewar America, since people who had lived in rural areas would be more likely to survive than the inhabitants of cities and suburbs. The surviving population would lack some key industrial and technical skills; on the other hand, rural people and those urban people who would survive are generally hardier than the American average.

While the absolute level of surviving stocks of materials and products would seem low by prewar standards, there would be a much smaller population to use these stocks. Apart from medicines (which tend to have a short shelf life and which are manufactured exclusively in urban areas), there would probably not be any essential commodity of which supplies were desperately short at first. A lack of medicines would accentuate the smallness and hardiness of the surviving population.

Restoring production would be a much more difficult task than finding interim stockpiles. Production in the United States is extremely complex, involving many intermediate stages. New patterns of production, which did not rely on facilities that have been destroyed, would have to be established.

It cannot be said whether the productive facilities that physically survived (undamaged or repairable with available supplies and skills) would be adequate to sustain recovery. It seems probable that there would be enough equipment and that scavenging among the ruins could provide adequate "raw materials" where natural resources were no longer accessible with surviving technology.

The most serious problems would be organizational. Industrial society depends on the division of labor, and the division of labor depends on certain governmental functions. Physical security comes first—a person is reluctant to leave home to go to work without some assurance that the home will not be looted. While some degree of law and order could probably be maintained in localities where a fairly dense population survived, the remaining highways might become quite unsafe, which would reduce trade over substantial distances. The second requirement is some form of payment for work. Barter is notoriously inefficient. Payment by fiat (for example, those who work get Government ration cards) is inefficient as well, and requires a Government stronger than a postwar United States would be likely to inherit. A strong Government might grow up, but most surviving citizens would be reluctant to support a dictatorship by whatever name. The best solution is a viable monetary system, but it would not be easy to establish. Regions or localities might develop their own monies, with "foreign" trade among regions.

The surviving resources might not be used very efficiently. Ideally one would want to conduct a national survey of surviving assets, but the surviving Government would probably not be capable of doing so, especially since people would fear that to acknowledge a surviving stock was to invite its confiscation. To make use of surviving factories, workers would have to live nearby, and they might be unwilling to do so in the absence of minimally adequate housing for their families. Ownership of some assets would be hopelessly confused, which would diminish the incentives for investment or even temporary repairs.

There is a possibility that the country might break up into several regional entities. If these came into conflict with each other there would be further waste and destruction.

In effect, the country would enter a race, with economic viability as the prize. The country would try to restore production to the point where consumption of stocks and the wearing out of surviving goods and tools was matched by new production. If this was achieved before stocks ran out, then viability would be attained. Otherwise, consumption would necessarily sink to the level of new production and in so doing would probably depress production further, creating a downward spiral. At some point this spiral would stop, but by the time it did so the United States might have returned to the economic equivalent of the Middle Ages.

The effect of an all-out attack would be equally devastating to the U.S. social structure. Heavy fatalities in the major urban areas would deprive the country of a high percentage of its top business executives, Government officials, medical specialists, scientists, educators, and performers. There is no measure for estimating the impact of such lasting losses on our society. In addition to the irreplaceable loss of genius and talents, the destruction of their associated institutions is still another compounding of effects that is overlooked by some recovery estimates. Who could calculate how long to get over the loss of Wall Street, an MIT, a Mayo Clinic, and the Smithsonian?

The American way of life is characterized by material possessions, with private ownership of items representing substantial long-term investments (such as homes, businesses, and automobiles) being the rule rather than exception. Widespread loss of individual assets such as these could have a strong, lasting effect on our social structure. Similarly, the question of whether individual right to ownership of surviving assets would remain unchanged in a post-attack environment would arise. For example, the Government might find it necessary to force persons having homes to house families who had lost their homes.

The family group would be particularly hard hit by the effects of general nuclear war. Deaths, severe injuries, forced separation, and loss of contact could place inordinate strains on the family structure.

Finally, major changes should be anticipated in the societal structure, as survivors attempt to adapt to a severe and desponding environment never before experienced. The loss of a hundred million people, mostly in the larger cities, could raise a question on the advisability of rebuilding the cities. (Why reconstruct obvious targets for a nuclear Armageddon of the future?) The surviving population could seek to alter the social and geopolitical structure of the rebuilding nation in hopes of minimizing the effects of any future conflicts.

How well the U.S. political structure might recover from a large-scale nuclear attack depends on a number of uncertainties. First, with warning, national level officials are presumed to evacuate to outlying shelter areas; State and local authorities will take similar precautions, but probably with less success, especially at the lower levels. The confidence and credibility of the system will come under severe strains as relief and recovery programs are implemented. Changes in an already weakened structure are sure to result as many normal practices and routines are set aside to facilitate recovery. Survivors may demand more immediate expressions of their likes, dislikes, and needs. Widespread dissatisfaction could result in a weakening of the Federal process, leading to a new emphasis on local government. An alternative possibility is martial law, which might be controlled in theory but decentralized in practice.*

---

*All of this assumes that there would be no significant ecological damage, a possibility discussed elsewhere in the report.

IV.

Ban the Bomb

1980s

In addition to the problem of nuclear proliferation, nuclear testing was also a concern. Open-air testing from the late 1940s to the early 1960s pushed radioactive particles high into the atmosphere, and monitoring these particles allowed meteorologists to trace upper-atmosphere wind patterns. These studies led to concerns about the long-term effects of open-air testing on public health. One of the leaders on this issue was Linus Pauling, a prominent American chemist. He had declined to work on the Manhattan Project and after the war became a vocal opponent of further development of nuclear weapons. After becoming a Nobel laureate in chemistry in 1954 for his work on chemical bonds, he grew more aggressive in his antinuclear activities, earning considerable suspicion from the federal government and some other scientists that he was a communist sympathizer. His 1958 book, *No More War!*, emphasized his pacifist convictions. Concerned about the accumulation of radioactive fallout in the atmosphere, Pauling campaigned for the United States and Soviet Union to at least stop open-air testing in the interest of public health. His efforts helped lead to the 1963 Nuclear Test-Ban Treaty, and he received the 1962 Nobel Peace Prize, the only person to win two undivided Nobel Prizes and only one of three to ever win two Nobel Prizes at all.

After the world began to recognize the environmental damage that resulted from open-air testing, testing moved underground, where the fallout and radiation would be trapped. The Americans and Soviets signed the Partial Test-Ban Treaty in October 1963, a year to the month after the Cuban Missile Crisis. Getting other nations to stop testing took longer. Until nuclear testing was abandoned in 1992, the Americans exploded 1,030 test weapons (215 atmospheric and 815 underground). The Soviet Union exploded 715 tests (219 atmospheric and 496 underground). France exploded 210 tests (50 atmospheric and

160 underground) and was the last of the original nuclear club to abandon nuclear testing in 1996. Britain was more frugal, conducting only 45 tests (21 atmospheric and 24 underground). China also conducted only 45 tests (23 atmospheric and 22 underground), the last in 1996. Other nations have conducted underground tests only.

While many people saw the preservation of nations ensured by nuclear weapons, other people were terrified of nuclear weapons in any form. A massive "Ban the Bomb" peace movement developed in the early 1980s, concentrated in Western Europe, though there were protests and political efforts in America also. The aggressive rhetoric of the Reagan Administration had alarmed and irritated the peace activists. The decision by the Americans to deploy the neutron bomb and Pershing II short-range missile into European bases, enhancing the American ability to fight a tactical nuclear war instead of immediately escalating to a strategic war, also angered Europeans. They saw Europe as the potential battleground between the two superpowers, and Europeans would be the main victims, especially in a tactical nuclear war. The neutron bomb was particularly horrifying in that it was a tactical nuclear weapon designed to enhance the short-term radiation effects of the nuclear explosion and minimize the blast effects. Part of the rationale for developing the neutron bomb was that it could be used in Europe during a war and would reduce the collateral damage to friendly countries. The bomb was truly a people killer. The persistence of the peace activists failed to get major changes in NATO nuclear policies. Some scholars have argued, considering the ideological intensity of the Cold War between the democracies and communism, that the fear of MAD and nuclear weapons actually prevented a third world war.

In the 1980s, the prominent astronomer and science popularizer Carl Sagan and other researchers concluded that a massive exchange of nuclear weapons between the Soviet Union and United States, as envisioned by MAD, would not only kill millions, but the dust raised by the explosions would drop the world's temperature and lead to a "nuclear winter." Sagan came to this conclusion after he noticed that temperatures on Mars had dropped during a massive dust storm observed by an orbiting Mariner spacecraft. When one of the nuclear reactors at Chernobyl caught fire in 1986, the widespread radiation and permanent evacuation of the surrounding area reminded people that any sort of nuclear war would be an awful environmental catastrophe.

While still furiously building more nuclear and biological weapons, the Soviet Union slowly crumbled in the 1980s. Its economy had been stagnant since the 1970s, and only the sale of oil in world markets kept the nation financially viable. An American plan to glut the world oil market with Saudi oil, driving down the price, led to a severe shortage of hard currency in the Soviet Union. Mikhail Gorbachev, a vigorous reformer, came to power in 1985 and enacted many quick changes to revitalize the Soviet economy and its political system. Instead of looking on the Eastern European satellite nations as national security assets, he saw them as economic burdens. He also made it obvious that he had no stomach for violence to maintain communism. Once he showed that he was different than his predecessors in this regard, the people of Eastern Europe rapidly discarded their governments in 1989. East German citizens literally tore down the Berlin Wall, graphically symbolizing that everything had changed. In 1991, the Soviet Union itself dissolved into its constituent republics, and the Cold War ended.

A generation has passed since then. When I teach my college students about nuclear weapons and the Cold War, most of them cannot quite grasp the umbrella of terror created by the MAD-induced standoff between the superpowers. The collapse of the Soviet Union is just a fact of life for them, while to this historian it was completely astonishing. The Soviet Union was very much a successor to the Russian Empire, and for a multiethnic empire to just vote itself out of existence, with minimum violence, stunned those of us who study history and know that normally empires are born and die in blood. A novelist could not have written a more surprising ending to the Cold War.

The United States and Russia signed the Comprehensive Nuclear Test-Ban Treaty in 1996, as did many other nations. This stopped all nuclear testing by the signatories, though some emerging nuclear powers have not signed it. A collection of scholars estimated that the United States spent $5.8 trillion on nuclear weapons from 1940 to 1996 (adjusted to 1996 dollars). In the end, the bombing of Hiroshima and Nagasaki is the only time nuclear weapons have been used in war.

We hope it remains that way.

Appendix
Shall We Play a Game?

As the American involvement in the Vietnam War reached its height in 1967, the Pentagon did not forget its other responsibilities. The Soviets, stung by their humiliation during the Cuban Missile Crisis, were pouring enormous resources into building up their nuclear forces. That year the Joint War Games Agency at the Pentagon organized two politico-military games, Beta I and Beta II, in order to help senior decision makers better understand a world in which the U.S. dominance in nuclear weapons had changed. The Blue team represented the United States, and the Red team represented the Soviet Union. Each Red and Blue team had fifty participants forming an action-level team (the equivalent of middle-management in rank from lieutenant colonel to major general) and a thirty-two member senior-level team (including full generals and their equivalent from many departments in the federal government). A team captain ran each team, and one of the captains was a professor from Harvard, Henry A. Kissinger. A Control team managed the game and represented other nations. Many of the details of these games remain classified, but what has been declassified presents intriguing portrayals of possible threats.

BETA I

The main difference between the two scenarios is that in Beta I the United States no longer has overwhelming strategic nuclear superiority. The Americans still have more nuclear warheads and launchers, but the Soviets have deployed an anti-ballistic missile (ABM) system. The Americans and Soviets are essentially at parity. NATO is crumbling as France, Italy, and Iceland withdraw from the organization. As Cold War tensions increase in Europe, the East German army seizes West Berlin in a single night of operations in 1972. Two American photo-reconnaissance satellites are destroyed by a new technology, Soviet anti-satellite weapons. War breaks out as NATO forces try to recover West Berlin. Tactical nuclear weapons are used, then strategic nuclear weapons come into play. Neither side wants war, but the weaker Red team had acted boldly, escalating the situation until it spun out of control. While it is not clear from the documents, apparently the Red team felt that it must launch a first nuclear strike on the United States.

BETA II

The second scenario is also set five years in the future in 1972. The United States has retained strategic nuclear superiority, while both sides have deployed ABM systems. The Americans have won the Vietnam War and even expelled Castro from Cuba. The participants were presented with a cascading set of problems, beginning with West Germany (FRG) building their own nuclear weapons. The West Germans want their own nuclear deterrent, just as Britain and France already have. The Soviets react by resuming open air testing, a violation of their treaties. Only three decades earlier, Germany had savaged the Soviet Union during World War II, and the idea of the West Germans acquiring nuclear weapons touches deep fears with the Soviet psyche. The Western allies are also not impressed by the West German nuclear armament decision.

The Soviets and their Warsaw Pact allies escalate the situation by mobilizing their strategic and conventional forces in Europe, and declaring a selective blockade of West Berlin. Civilian supplies are cut off to the West German population, but treaty rights for the military units of the former occupying powers (U.S., British, and French) are not interfered with. The Soviets effectively use propaganda and diplomatic efforts to isolate West Germany and define the problem as only a problem with West Germany. They also launch an air strike to destroy the West German nuclear program. This attack is mostly successful, but the Soviets fear that West German nuclear weapons are still available. The Soviets plan that if a West German nuclear weapon is used, they will retaliate with three nuclear weapons of their own, but only against West Germany. They will warn the United States to stop West Germany, since the Soviets will not allow their nuclear resources to be bled by the West Germans while the United States stands aside and is not damaged. An assumption of the Beta II game is that a first nuclear strike by the Soviets would cause 20 million to 30 million American casualties, while 30 million to 50 million Soviets would be killed or wounded by the inevitable American retaliatory strike. A first nuclear strike by the Americans would kill or wound 100 million to 120 million Soviets, while the Soviet counterstrike would lead to 5 million to 10 million American casualties.

Faced with a lack of support from their NATO allies, West Germany agrees to halt the German nuclear program. Just after the European crisis comes to a resolution, China and North Korea attack South Korea. American and South Korean conventional forces cannot repel the onslaught and ask for permission to use tactical nuclear weapons. The Chinese threaten to use their own nuclear weapons if the Americans use theirs. This was the first war game ever run by the Pentagon that included the recent development of Chinese nuclear weapons. How this game ended is still classified.

In reality, the West Germans never developed their own nuclear weapons because they expected the consequences might be similar to the above scenario. A major purpose of these games was to analyze the impact of ABM systems, but much of the content on that aspect of the game was redacted, making it difficult to see how these games might have affected the later American decision to seek a treaty banning ABM systems. The National Security Advisor during the negotiation and signing of the ABM Treaty and key figure in all aspects of the Soviet-American relationship during the Nixon and Ford administrations was former game captain Henry A. Kissinger.

Index